ACTING IN COMMERCIALS

SECOND EDITION

ACTING IN COMMERCIALS

A Guide to Auditioning and Performing On Camera

JOAN SEE

BACK STAGE BOOKS

An imprint of Watson-Guptill Publications, New York

To my students, past and present

First edition published in 1993 by Back Stage Books, an imprint of Watson-Guptill Publications, a division of VNU Business Media, Inc., 770 Broadway, New York, NY 10003-9595 www.watsonguptill.com

This book was an editorial project of International Screen, Television & Entertainment Literature, Inc.

Acquiring editor: Dale Ramsey
Book design: Jay Anning
Production manager: Hector Campbell
Illustrations: Ron Crawford

Library of Congress Cataloging-in-Publication Data
See, Joan
    Acting in commercials : a guide to auditioning and performing on camera / Joan See.
        p.   cm.
    Includes bibliographical references and index.
    ISBN 0-8230-8802-2
    1. Acting for television-Vocational guidance. 2. Television advertising-Vocational guidance. I. Title.
PN1992. 8. A3S441993
791. 45'028'025-dc20

Manufactured in the United States of America

4 5 6 7 8 9 / 08 07 06 05 04

Acknowledgments

Writing is a humbling experience. As I recall the many sources of support I have required putting this book together, I realize how truly grateful I am for the journey that other acting teachers have taken before me: I am indebted to the work of Stella Adler and Uta Hagen for their succinct expression of the mysteries of acting; and Michael Caine's insights on the camera-actor relationship reveal him to be more than just another accomplished movie actor. However, there is no way I would have been able to successfully work with actors if it had not been for the great Sanford Meisner. As a teacher, he always sought to solve the actor's individual problem, and in doing so, he found new ways to teach us all. The concept of the "reality of doing", one of the foundations of the Meisner approach, was a lesson I learned from Sandy long ago. It is a lesson that has never failed me in the moment of the test. It is the cornerstone of everything I know about acting.

Fine minds, great teachers, and excellent performers have touched my life and enriched my teaching. In particular, Richard Fonda and Mike Miller were wonderful actors and teachers; I miss them both. And my time spent on the Screen Actors Guild Board of Directors widened my knowledge of the business of this craft beyond measure.

The faculty of The School for Film and Television are a special group indeed. Their care and commitment to the actors of the future has always been the key ingredient of our success. They have shared with me their accumulated wisdom and vision. Without them, I could not have persevered. And when it comes to vision, creativity, and contribution to the School for Film and Television, Jack Newman's commitment to its development went a long way toward making it happen. And, of course, my love is always with the other two of Three of Us Corporation. When I didn't think I could make a future happen I found strength in my commitment to them.

As I ventured on this writing road, I needed to find courage. I owe affection and gratitude to Sonny Stokes for helping me find the map to it, and Casey Kelly, who has not only been my friend, but an inspiring example of writing discipline and bravery. I deeply appreciate the understanding and patience of my beloved agents at Cunningham, Escott, Dipene, particularly Ken Slevin and Carrie Morgan. They have always supported and encouraged me. When it comes to patience, John Istel, my editor, should win a prize.

There is no conservatory, studio, school, or theater without management. Behind the people who are center stage there are those who make it all possible. This industry is called show business not show art. David Palmer is the person who keeps The School for Film and Television shipshape, and he does it brilliantly. It would have been impossible for me to take this time to write if David and my school administrator, Marc Aronin, had not created an opportunity for me to be away from The School for days at a time. A young man of remarkable talents, Marc has also served as test reader and cheering section. My other cheering section, the illustrator and artist Ron Crawford, is the fastest and most wonderful collaborator any writer could have. Thank you, friends!

CONTENTS

Introduction

There have been a number of books written about commercials. The majority fall into the "you-too-can-be-a-star" genre. They aim to introduce the total beginner to the so-called glamorous world of commercials. They guide the reader through a general survey course in commercial acting, offering lessons in everything from "What Is a Casting Director?" to "Getting Your Pet into Commercials." The best of these provide a nice overview of the industry and an introduction to the basics.

This book definitely does not take a "you-too . . ." approach. It was never my desire to imitate the way that some people initiate the novice actor into this industry. I write from experience. I have lived through almost all of the feelings and frustrations regarding acting and auditioning for commercials that I discuss in this book. My training, first as an actor, and second as a successful actor in commercials, has given me a perspective different from most. (I should say here that I prefer to call all performers "actors" regardless of gender; after all, there are no doctoresses or pilotesses, and though there are waitresses, most of them are actors anyway.)

Years ago, when I began to teach, I decided to teach what I knew. I knew about an acting process; I didn't know magic tricks. I knew that my acting technique had always been the place to which I returned when everything else about performing seemed bewildering. I also knew that the directors and actors whom I respected in the business of making television commercials were craftspeople and artists. By working with such professionals, I learned how to adapt to and survive in what I first experienced as a hostile world.

In the old days, there was often time on a set to talk about acting and commercial film techniques with the director and crew. Likewise, agents had time to guide actors and explain the business to them. By the time I started teaching, most of that had changed.

It is easy to forget that the television industry is young and fast-moving. When I began in 1962, commercials had been organized by Screen Actors Guild for only two years. The golden age of the commercial had just begun. The golden goose had just begun to lay the golden eggs. What had started quietly in the 1950s had become a multibillion-dollar culture-shaping enterprise by the 1980s. Actors were as eager and vulnerable as ever, but now they were under siege in a pressured business climate that coldly used up new faces and only wanted more. Because so much money was being spent in the filming and broadcasting of television commercials, test marketing ruled what spots got on the air. Every client wanted the biggest market share they could get for the dollars they invested. Casting was considered critical. The pressure to find the "right" actor lead to casting by committee. Everyone had to have a say, and if the group couldn't agree on "the one" from a pool of twenty auditioning actors, then maybe a larger pool of forty might solve the deadlock.

On the set, there was no time for the creative people to sit around and share trade secrets. The set was jammed with people from all levels of the process, and the director as well as the ad execs were under the scrutiny of the ever-critical client. Everyone guarded his or her secrets well—they didn't give it away anymore. In the offices and on the sets, the time needed to "take time" for actors vanished. The lessons I learned from my peers were no longer so easily come by. Actors came into the commercial world eager to book and make money but were abandoned without a life jacket to the swirling waters of "do it right," "do it now," and maintain your sense of humor, no matter what.

Nevertheless, everyone—from agents to the untried performers—had this idea that performing in commercials was easy. It never seems to have dawned on them that the actors made it look that way.

As television advertising became more complex, the actors' need for guidance grew as well. To meet their needs, there has been a profusion of classes that offer actors general information about the business and give them a chance to see themselves on-camera. Most of these classes are taught by casting directors. Serious and nonserious performers alike pay large amounts of money to take these workshops as a way of meeting important professionals. Unfortunately, many of these classes only help advance the mistaken conception that anyone can do the job and no real technique is required.

Most casting directors are very good at what they do—casting. But because of the nature of their profession, they have been, and remain, result-oriented teachers. There's nothing wrong with that—it's the way casting directors should be. They understand what kind of performers they need in order to get the result that their client is looking for. Yet, in most cases, their approach doesn't begin to address the techniques necessary to get such a castable performance. Most of them, even if they were actors at one time, have never had to produce bookable results in the pressure-packed atmosphere of the commercial audition and callback. Casting directors have a great deal to offer actors in commercials after those actors have received an acting foundation. Then, actors can really utilize the insights these professionals have to offer.

For a long time, performers with performance problems in commercials had nowhere to turn. No one was working with trained actors in a process-oriented way, a way that enabled them to use their training. As an actor, I understood their dilemma, and I decided to teach commercial performing through the acting technique I already knew.

My approach has been extremely successful. My students have gone out into the marketplace and worked. My experience with this kind of training has shown me that not only does the commercial work of my students improve, but also there is an immediate and equally exciting improvement in their "legitimate" acting endeavors. Because the commercial form compresses the story and the closeness of the camera's eye allows for no phony dramatics, bad habits have no place to hide. As a result of studying with me, actors often get rid of these habits and find a new honesty and simplicity in their work.

This book condenses the acting methods that have yielded such helpful results for so many. Be warned, however, that like any skill, mastering the information in this book takes time and practice. This is not a quick-fix manual.

I hope that all talented people involved in commercial production read this book. Anything that fosters an easier and more productive partnership between actor and production team should be encouraged. We all want to produce the same thing: quality commercials and repeat business. This book offers directors a language with which to talk to actors. It also provides techniques that can help them coax a performance from talent on the set.

This is a book about acting and, specifically, about acting in television commercials—acting that must be quick, but that is not necessarily easy.

Part One
WORKING IN COMMERCIALS

1

Why Actors Need Commercials

A good stage actor can act in films.
PETER BROOK

Not too long ago, a manager called me for help with a new client. She had just signed a beautiful and, in the manager's opinion, talented young woman. Because she was being sent to commercial auditions, the manager wanted to be sure that her client was able to compete successfully. I arranged for the young woman to meet with me at my studio and invited her manager to join us. The manager was delighted: She had never seen her client on-camera, even though she was trying to get her auditions for feature film roles.

I asked the young woman (let's call her Jane) to be prepared to do a monologue as well as read some commercial copy. When they arrived, it was obvious that the manager had not been mistaken about Jane's beauty. She was as lovely as the manager's description had promised. Nevertheless, Jane shared her manager's concern about her commercial technique. She told me that the whole process mystified her; and though she was an extremely well-trained actor, she had no idea how to handle commercial copy. She told me she felt lost and intimidated in front of a camera.

I gave Jane several cue cards and asked her to select one that she thought she could relate to. She chose a commercial about a young woman coping with city life. Then Jane stepped to the mark, and I started the camera. She slated herself and began to read the copy. (See the glossary for terms that may be unfamiliar.)

To describe Jane's delivery as wooden would be too kind. She clasped her hands tightly behind her back, put all of her weight on one foot, and her body remained rigid from the neck down. Her jaw and mouth were tense, and as she worked to pronounce the words, she thrust her mouth unattractively. Her performance seemed to indicate that Jane's manager had been mistaken about her client's talent.

Then I asked Jane to do her monologue. She sat in a chair and took time to settle and center herself. When she began, it seemed as if a different actress had appeared in front of the camera. Her body didn't sit stiffly in the chair but draped itself over the arms and curled in the seat. She was vividly present and alive in the moment. She spoke with a voice that readily reflected her inner life, and her words conveyed meaningful thoughts. This Jane knew what she was talking about. The previous Jane simply read the words off the card and hoped that sheer force of expression would communicate. Why had her acting disappeared in her commercial performance?

DANGEROUS PRECONCEPTIONS

As Jane, her manager, and I grappled with this question, several things became clear. Her mock commercial audition was Jane's first experience in front of a camera. The camera itself was intimidating; she could only see it for its metal, plastic, and glass components. And yet the copy demanded that she relate and talk to it as if it were a person. The camera watched her like an audience in a theater, but unlike a live audience it never disappeared into the dark as the lights went down.

To complicate matters, Jane was very aware that the camera shot was a medium close-up. Although the camera was about thirteen feet from her, she knew the picture in the monitor only showed us her face and upper body. She allowed this notion to box her in physically. The fact that we were only seeing a portion of her seemed to deprive Jane of the right to use the rest of herself, and she died from the neck down. In her mind, the plastic perimeter of the nineteen-inch television monitor was an impenetrable boundary. As much as she felt free and expansive in filling theatrical space, she felt squeezed into the monitor's picture. It seemed to demand that her performance be small, restrained, and pulled-back. These preconceptions were responsible for shutting down Jane's on-camera performance.

More troubling, Jane's uninformed notions about on-camera acting had the potential to sabotage her film and television auditions as well. Sooner or later in the film-casting process, actors encounter the taped audition. This type of audition usually occurs after the actor has met and read for the casting director. If the actor has given a good reading and is physically right for the part, the actor is asked to memorize a scene and come back and be recorded on videotape. At that audition, the casting director or a hired reader will stand behind the camera and read the other character's lines. The actor will be expected to respond to the camera, treating the machine as if it were a scene partner. If Jane were to get a callback for a film and applied her small, pulled-back ideas of on-camera acting to it, her audition would be in danger of being as awkward and strangulated as the simulated commercial audition she had done for me.

Many actors share Jane's uninitiated viewpoint. They feel constrained by the supposed limitations of the camera's framing and, therefore, believe that just being smaller or doing less will result in good film acting.

ACTING, NOT SELLING

Beyond the problems of the camera, Jane's preconceptions about the whole medium of television commercial advertising further sabotaged her ability to succeed. They prevented her from treating the commercial copy as a dramatic script; otherwise she would have applied her most basic acting techniques to the process.

Unfortunately, Jane presumed that acting in commercials wasn't "real" acting, that it was something different. She believed that the difference lay in what the auditioners wanted her to do. She believed that they wanted her to sell a product. Selling was the job, and Jane knew that selling was not what she had been trained to do.

Moreover, Jane suspected that the commercial audition was a total crapshoot: Commercials were not about any kind of craft—they were only about how she looked. Since she assumed working in commercials did not require any skill or craft, Jane experienced no sense of control. There was nothing she could do. Her feeling of powerlessness only exacerbated her normal performance anxiety. As an actor in a television commercial, Jane felt like a decoration at best and a used-car seller at worst.

In addition, the script was so short and the audition so fast that the experience seemed like quicksilver—an ordeal that she could neither capture nor examine. No wonder Jane felt lost and intimidated. Her predicament was completely understandable, considering her lack of camera experience, her misconceptions, and her anxiety.

Jane's hangups about acting in commercials are common among actors— and toxic. The first thing she and others like her need to understand is the concept of *on-camera acting*. Until they understand how acting on-camera is like acting onstage and how it is different, their auditions in front of a camera may be as terrified, wooden, and unconvincing as Jane's trial attempt in my studio.

THE REWARDS

If the idea of doing a commercial audition was so painful, why were Jane and her manager spending so much time and energy evaluating her potential for success? The answer is simple: money. It might be months before Jane landed a film or television role that paid enough for her to devote herself full-time to the business of acting. In the meantime, she had to pay for pictures, résumés, classes, clothes, and the general costs of living. Booking several network commercials would provide the capital for her professional war chest.

Many actors working in commercials view the medium as a means to an end. There's nothing wrong with that idea. Commercials pay the rent, pay for classes, make regional theater roles affordable, and help actors live like other people. All these motives are absolutely fine. Actors and advertisers have a terrific symbiotic relationship. Advertisers use actors and their talents as one of the components of their sales campaigns. Actors use the financial reward for such service to support careers and families.

The facts about employment in our craft have always been disheartening. The generally accepted unemployment figure for the three major acting unions—Actors' Equity Association (AEA), Screen Actors Guild (SAG), and the American Federation of Television and Radio Artists (AFTRA)—runs around eighty-five percent of their membership. As limited as jobs have always been in the theater, the situation has worsened over the last decade. Escalating production costs have forced the closure of many summer stock and dinner theaters. Only twenty-four dinner theaters in the country pay union wages—and that average salary is only $300 to $400 a week before deductions.

Regional theaters have suffered as well. Reductions in the monies available from grant sources and civic subsidies, plus increased production costs, have conspired to make the job of creating theater more difficult. The theaters that have managed to stay afloat are operating on tighter budgets with reduced seasons, and are choosing plays with smaller casts.

Although some of the best theater is happening in the regions, the best salaries are not. The average regional theater salary is $525 per week. Even if this includes lodging, after actors subtract their agent's commission and withholding taxes and take one deduction, on the average they pocket a grand sum of $322.50. This barely supports the cost of living.

Off-off Broadway theater companies generally pay nothing. In fact, actors usually pay to be part of the cast. They share the cost of advertising and mailings, buy props and costumes, and sometimes share the cost of renting the theater. Actors working off-Broadway average $600 per week, and understudies on Broadway in a drama make $1,090, minimum, per week according to Equity scale. The old pros that shake their heads in waiting rooms all over New York and moan that you can't make a living in the theater any longer are right. You can't!

In order to survive today, actors need to be able to perform in any and all performance mediums. They must abandon any notions of specializing in only one field. I like to call this diversification. Although an overwhelming number of actor training institutions continue to educate their students exclusively for the theater, the reality is that the actor who can't take that training and use it in front of a camera may not survive in the business. Today, a successful career requires that actors move effortlessly and effectively from a play to a commercial, to a soap opera, to a film—and back again.

Economic realities force performers—like Jane—to come to grips with a simple fact: It is necessary to work on-camera, particularly in commercials. It pays well. Salaries and fees paid in radio and television commercials and programming have always outstripped fees paid for purely theatrical endeavors. In 1996, SAG contracts awarded its members more than $1.4 billion; in contrast, AEA's membership earned $212.5 million, 15 percent of SAG's total. But what should really surprise most actors is that in 1996 commercials accounted for about $448 million of the total earnings of SAG members, while theatrical feature films—the movies everyone is trying to break into—paid out nearly $408 million, or about 40 million less. And that figure includes stars' salaries of millions per picture. In other words, commercials make more than twice as much money for performers as Equity's combined annual earnings and a third more than SAG feature films.

The reasons commercials have historically paid actors so much money are not difficult to understand. Because communication through sound and light waves provided a mass audience of potential consumers, it was the answer to an advertiser's prayers. Mass audiences meant mass markets and the mass market promised mass sales. The profits from these mass sales have encouraged and enabled advertisers to highly reward those who create and deliver their advertising messages.

For that reason, the value placed upon on-camera actors' abilities grows in direct proportion to the value that can be accrued in the marketplace through the use of those abilities. Large market shares, high TVQs, good ratings, and great test-market results are the things of which paychecks are made. Simply stated: Commercial radio and television programs are designed to get an audience's attention so that they can be exposed to an advertiser's message. The creative team that can get and keep that attention is highly valued by the companies whose products they are advertising. Whether that creative team is creating a commercial or a program, the goal is the same.

However, the idea that all commercial television is ruled by this central fact doesn't seem to enter into the thinking of actors as they strive to land a role on a soap, a pilot, or a sitcom. They may be aware that contract-holding newcomers on a one-hour soap can be guaranteed a minimum of $800 for one show. But they perceive that salary as a reward for the performance rather than for a performance that sells soap. Because they never mention the product during their time on screen, they assume it has nothing to do with them. They forget that the genre is called *soap* opera—so-called because soap manufacturers such as Proctor & Gamble pay for the production as a hook onto which they hang their advertisements. Should the audience defect and the ratings falter, for whatever reason, the program could disappear, no matter how good the individual performers may be.

Understanding the marketplace mindset of broadcasting is vital to the actor who wishes to flourish via the TV screen, and this is particularly true for commercials. Knowledge and acceptance of the way the medium works, and why it works that way, prepares an actor to cooperate with its needs. For actors to reap the monetary benefits available, they must be clear about what is required. Then they must be prepared to deliver it.

So what does this all mean for poor Jane? Is there any hope? Absolutely! Jane is a good actress. That she doesn't show it when reading commercial copy is a function of her ignorance about the commercial form and its requirements, her lack of knowledge about how the camera sees, and the absence of an acting technique specific to this medium.

If Jane believes she can be trained to work in the movies, then she certainly can be trained to work in television's "mini advertising movies," which is what I often call commercials. Jane can learn how to book commercials and get residual checks without compromising her theatrical background. Such training will give her an opportunity to see the camera as friendly. Although the camera has made her painfully aware that she needs remedial work on her breathing and facial tension, the camera told her the truth, revealing problems that, for whatever reason, her previous teachers had let pass. The camera never lies, and in all likelihood it will be the most perceptive teacher Jane has ever had.

The news is good not only for Jane, but for the majority of actors who come from theatrical backgrounds. Most of them share Jane's crippling preconceptions and feelings about commercials, as well as her lack of camera experience. Their inability to book commercials is often a devastating psychological blow to egos already embattled by a difficult business. A little good information often has remarkable results.

For more than fifteen years I have been working with actors, giving them a process, informing them about what advertisers need, and allowing them an opportunity to practice new ways of doing this work. I am happy to report that I have turned many careers around. Not only have my students' commercial performances improved, but their work in "legit" projects has blossomed as well.

While this book shares my accumulated experiences, information, ideas, and techniques, I do not claim to have invented anything new. Rather, I have organized and applied some time-tested truths in different ways. The result is a technique for acting in commercials.

Notice I didn't write "commercial acting"; I wrote "acting in commercials." Acting is a craft with a foundation of basic skills. Just because actors use their craft in front of a camera instead of on a stage doesn't change the foundation of their technique. It changes the kind of structure that will be built on top of it. Here's an analogy: a farmhouse, a townhouse, and an apartment house all have foundations that use the same rules of engineering. However, each type of house fits the needs of the occupants and the environment in which it is built. None of them will stand long without that strong foundation.

My technique for acting in commercials is all about applying the general rules of our craft—the foundation—to a specific medium and type of text. These are the basic acting skills that seasoned actors are supposed to know already. They are the same skills that talented beginners need to learn—and quickly.

2

What Is a Television Commercial?

*The goal of every communication is duplication. You want
the other person to think as you do, to repeat what you have
just said, to feel what you feel, to agree with you.*

MICHAEL SHURTLEFF

Most people do not know much about television commercials beyond the fact
that they are designed to sell products. They know even less about how commercials are produced and how they go about accomplishing their goals. Most
American television viewers probably don't know that commercials fill
approximately six out of every thirty minutes of television program time. They
also might be shocked to learn that the average commercial costs about
$189,000 to produce. Moreover, it is highly unlikely that the average viewer is
aware of the legion of specialists—ranging from food stylists to media buyers—who service the television commercial machine.

A SHORT HISTORY OF TV COMMERCIALS

By the time TV sets became a common sight in most American living rooms,
the tremendous marketing opportunities they promised already had begun to
boggle the minds of advertisers. As had previously happened with the advent
of radio, television moved advertising into the intimacy of people's homes.
However, this new medium offered pictures to go along with the words—
moving pictures. An industry was born.

In the early days, the majority of television commercials were performed
live, as were the programs they sponsored. Initially, these spots were between
sixty and ninety seconds in length and were rather like talking print ads.
Presenters—most often pretty young women—stood next to products and
gave little speeches about the outstanding qualities of the brands they represented. Sometimes, the presenter merely demonstrated the product while an
offstage voice described what the viewing audience saw.

There was little subtlety in the sell. A wise ad man once said, "Sex is the
baseline for a lot of people in America"; the image of a pretty young woman

has been a conventional and consistent means of getting an audience's attention. (Why do you think Thomas Edison put bathing beauties on his first reels of moving pictures?) The audience for these early ads was not meant to identify with the presenter. The commercial itself, even the few that were not live but prerecorded on film, were primarily designed to demonstrate the product's superior benefits. The advertiser's talent search focused on "models who could talk."

The job of the spokes-model wasn't easy. Rene Roy, spokes-model for DuPont, remembers the challenges:

> Coping with the changes in the copy was the hardest. You would memorize the copy you'd been given. However, between rehearsal and airing, or between same-day shows, the copy could be rewritten several times. I remember changes being given to me in a car ride between studios. They had cue cards, but I was afraid to use them. There was the fear that you would scramble the words plus the fear of not appearing believable.

As time passed, technology improved. Videotape enabled performances to be recorded. The ability to duplicate tape and replay the recorded material was a triumph for the television industry. It created all kinds of opportunities for programming. Television left behind the restrictions of the theater and gained the freedom of film. The new technology enabled on-camera commercials to be shot, post-produced on film, and then transferred to tape for broadcast. Anything that could be done in the movies could now be done on television and in commercials. The live spokes-model or presenter—even the taped one—was no longer a necessity, but a casting choice. Mini-entertainments could be created that sold the client's products in new and interesting ways. Therefore, actors who were trained to create a believable "somebody else" were needed. The era of holding up the product and smiling began to come to an end.

The ability to duplicate videotape changed everything. Not only were opportunities opened for actor and advertiser alike, but also the working relationship between the two changed. Because the new technology enabled advertisers to refine, freeze, and replicate a performance—so that once the actor-presenter recorded the commercial on tape it could be reused at any time—some real problems surfaced. Commercial producers loved it, of course; to them, one taping, many uses meant one taping fee and many free uses. Actors and announcers hated it for the same reason. Once they had been paid for the initial performance that created the master, the advertiser could duplicate it and use it forever at no additional charge.

A small group of New York leaders of the film union for actors, the Screen Actors Guild, addressed the problem. After a long struggle that included tense negotiations and even a strike, they created the contract that now provides more money to actors than feature films do. SAG's commercial contract, with its schedule of payment for re-use, lovingly called *residuals,* was a victory for the talent who had so consistently serviced the needs of the advertiser. Those residuals are the reason why performers turn to commercials as an avenue for income.

How Commercials Haven't Changed

The goal of the advertisers hasn't changed over the years. Their mission is still the same: getting the audience to think or feel in ways that motivate specific behavior. That specific behavior is the purchase or use of their product or service. Advertising, from packaging to print-ad, must effectively communicate with potential consumers. It does this by manipulating the consumers' perceptions and molding their desires.

Consider the carefully chosen colors found on the wrapping of a bar of soap. The blue and white wrapper on a bar of Ivory soap says virginal and pure, whereas the red and black wrapper on the bar of Lava leads us to perceive it as tough and strong. If I didn't read English and I had to choose the baby's bath soap from one of those two, which do you think I would select?

The medium that put moving and talking advertising pictures into people's homes offered advertisers potent tools of communication and persuasion, but it was not without its challenges. Television's first audiences were as large and diverse, economically as well as culturally, as they are today. Although the average American watches the tube six hours a day, viewers' attention to commercials can be fleeting. The escalating cost of television airtime has been partly responsible for "commercial shrinkage": Ads have become shorter in length and have multiplied in number. The sixty-second spot has become the twenty-eight-, the twenty-, or the fifteen-second spot. You now can put two or three commercials in the same time slot that used to be allotted to one. The challenge is to effectively communicate an advertising message amid many others.

Cable channels and remote-control channel-switching devices add to the difficulty of holding a viewer's attention. "Channel surfing" is an expression that has become part of the vernacular. The audience has become more visually sophisticated through its constant exposure to moving images. And the culture is constantly in a state of change.

Since 1957, when Vance Packard's book *The Hidden Persuaders* was published, the public has been increasingly aware of motivational research and the manipulation of perception. Unfortunately, the exploitation of our fears and fantasies as a means of shaping behavior has not become less pervasive since 1957, but more. Closely observe and analyze any recent political campaign and you'll see these strategies at work.

What has happened to those strategies over the years is that they have increased in use and become more sophisticated. An understanding of the subtleties of communication has been pioneered by the advertising industry. The compression of the television commercial story and the battle for each viewer's attention made it urgent that marketers fully understood not only what the viewer wanted in the products they purchased, but also, more importantly, why they wanted it. They also wanted to know exactly how the viewer responded to the smallest of details, from body language to hairstyles.

Advertisers' research easily discovered how consumers rated the actual benefits of a product, but, surprisingly, they found that these benefits were not always the most persuasive selling point. Finding out what really drives us to do the things we do, buy the products we buy, and continue buying them became the central focus of the advertisers' research. Spending millions of dollars to understand consumers' behavior, advertising researchers eventually saw that our *emotional responses* to a product are the key factors that attract and bind us to a particular brand. How we felt was as important as what we knew. Research then focused on how to create and strengthen these emotional bonds.

Armed with information on what benefits—both practical and emotional—a consumer expects from a product, creative advertising teams concoct commercials capable of pushing all the targeted viewers' buttons. They know exactly what feelings their clients' spots must generate in viewers in order to have success. They also know what feelings to avoid. Every creative detail is evaluated on its potential to elicit the desired response. Anything thought to be ambiguous is deleted.

That every element of a television ad must communicate with maximum efficiency affects all aspects of production, from the choice of director to casting to wardrobe. If the advertisement's creators have done their job well, the consumers should respond. If they do, the cycle of communication will be complete. The advertisers will have sent out their carefully crafted message. The consumers will have not only seen it and heard it but had an emotional response to it. They will have believed that Ruffles with Ridges are fun. In this agreement are the seeds of the sale.

The short time in which television advertisers must tell their stories has forced them to become master communicators. They get people to think and feel the way they do everyday, in twenty-eight seconds or less. The on-camera commercials they create are painstakingly crafted bits of film. Everything has been thought through on the basis of careful research, nothing has been left to chance—they've done their homework.

Advertisers are serious about getting results, and actors who want to be part of this industry had better get serious as well. Understanding how you fit into the commercial process and what is expected of you as a performer is the first step toward developing your technique.

ACTORS TELL, ADVERTISERS SELL

I often ask actors a simple question: "What do you think your job is in a commercial?" The answer I get: "To sell the product." It should be apparent from what you have just read that your job is not to sell.

The advertising agencies are responsible for selling goods and services. That is what they get paid to do. On-camera commercials are one of the ways that they go about doing it. And actors are one part of an army of profession-al craftspeople who are hired to carry out a plan for the production of an on-camera commercial. This collaboration is not unlike that which occurs in the theater. A script is written, producers are found. Designers, press agents, cast-ing directors and, finally, actors are hired to take the words of the script and make them believable to an audience. Actors bring the story to life.

The role of actors in commercials is similar. They must bring little stories to life in a way that makes other people believe them. However, no actor's per-formance can save an inferior product with a badly conceived and poorly executed marketing concept, any more than it can save a bad play.

That the actor's job is to tell the story, not sell the product, should make actors feel a sense of great relief and freedom. If you believe that your job is selling, you will think that something other than acting is required. You will be tempted to punch words and work to convince the audience of something you don't believe yourself. You will not be believable as a "real" person who had an experience with the product or service and, therefore, has feelings about it. So don't forget: *Advertisers hire you for your acting skills,* which enable you to communicate ideas and feelings in such a way that audiences will believe you. They are using your talent, just the way they're using the tal-ent of the cinematographer, the director, and the film editor.

The Problem of Speed

As an actor, however, you have a performance problem: Advertisers require that this communication happen in twenty-eight seconds or less. This com-pression of a story into such a short form means that actors must really under-stand which elements of their performance communicate ideas and feelings most effectively. Most actors have never even considered this question.

The first manifestation of this performance problem is the speed of the *audition* itself. You never get the script (or what they call *copy*) ahead of time. Usually, your agent can supply only minimal information. An agent's typical breakdown of commercial audition requirements might go something like this: "You're a Mom, kind of upscale-casual, and there's wall-to-wall copy." You get to see the copy only when you arrive at the audition, and the only time you have to prepare is between signing in and going into the studio.

Furthermore, the casting director does not speak an "acting language" that is familiar to most performers, and in the beginning that can be less than helpful. For example, a casting director described a commercial character that one of my students was auditioning for in the following way: "She's very bub-bly and fun, but with an edge. She's real and conversational. Maybe it's like you've been talking to your mother about something personal and this topic comes up. Okay, let's try it!" If you're lucky, you may get to do the material two or three times with new directions, such as, "Slow down," "Throw it away," or "Don't act."

The length of time you spend inside the casting studio may total four or five minutes. You leave with your mind a blur. Sometimes, during the elevator ride down to the street, you have a flash of insight, "That's what I should have done!" But it is too late.

ACTING AS COMMUNICATION

The only hope of avoiding such unsettling experiences is to understand the structure of commercials as thoroughly as possible. You want the ability to analyze copy quickly so that you know exactly what the story is about. This will enable you to understand what thoughts, ideas, and feelings need to be communicated. In the theater, this part of the acting process is called *script analysis*. That step leads to the next one: applying your acting technique to the task of communicating those ideas and feelings. Every acting choice, every performance detail must support, enhance, and expand the writer's message.

The first issue to be dealt with is the idea of communication. Michael Shurtleff feels strongly enough about the subject to remind actors about it in his book *Audition*. His "Guidepost 7" describes the process of acting as "supremely a task of communication." And he didn't mean "just talking."

I assume that Shurtleff's experience correlates with mine. Working with actors from all kinds of backgrounds has led me to believe that too many of them think that feeling is acting. Where has this idea come from? Perhaps the training programs that emphasize psychological investigation and a freeing of the emotions. You can have all the emotions in the world, yet if you can't access them at will and then, most importantly, communicate them—send them out to someone else—they don't mean a thing. You can't have them and hoard them. You have to have them and then give them away. "The most successful actors," says Shurtleff, "are those who are able to project what they are feeling to someone else."

The need to let someone else know how you are feeling leads to its projection. It is that feeling projected to another that is the "ping" of the communication circle. You send feelings to people in order to have an impact on them. You need them to listen and hear. Their response is the "pong." This circle of communication is called by many names: Ping-Pong, Pinch-Ouch, or—the best description of all—Action-Reaction.

For many actors, the idea of sending ideas and feelings away from themselves is very liberating. Self-absorption and passivity give way to energy and action. The benefits to their work are enormous. If acting is doing, then they have begun to do something. Projecting your feelings and ideas to someone else is doing. This ability to project feelings is crucial for the actor in commercials. Just thinking about how you feel is not enough; the camera—the viewer—has to receive and understand them.

How do we communicate or project our feelings? Like good advertisers, we need to know. Here's where I ask my students the next big question: "What is it that communicates to your partner or to your audience?" Eight out of ten times I get the wrong answer: "The words".

Part Two
Acting Fundamentals for Commercials

3

Communicating Without Words

When your attention is on the words, you worry mostly about yourself.

STELLA ADLER

Words are wonderful things. They come in two forms: the ones we write and the ones we speak. It is hard to conceive of communication without them, particularly the ones we speak. However, words are one of the later developments in the evolution of human communication. Before words were ever uttered, we communicated. We used nonverbal means.

Nonverbal communication occurs without the use of words, but not without the use of sound. Words are, of course, made of sound, and sound is the result of the way the physical body behaves. Nonverbal communication begins the moment your body consciously responds to your thoughts. What is going on in your mind begins to be made known to those around you through the way your body behaves. Your eye movements, your body language, the look on your face, all serve to create a picture book that is easily read and understood. If the body is compelled to make sound, the sound that the body makes will communicate volumes about the nature of the thought.

We communicate by other nonverbal means as well. What we wear and how we decorate ourselves transmit subtle, but powerful, messages. The image that is created solidifies our own sense of self for ourselves. One of the other purposes of that image is to identify ourselves to others. Our choices show others who we are, establish our status, and clearly communicate our cultural niche.

NONVERBAL COMMUNICATION

What we see is very powerful. Of our five senses, sight is the most highly developed. We learn most of what we know about the world around us through what we see.

From the first day that we focused our infant eyes, we started storing pictures in our brains. Addressing the actor, Michael Shurtleff points out that "we see our entire lives in pictures" and that our memories are stored visually. Think about a past event and you will remember it as a picture that has you in the middle of the scene. You can see your environment and the other participants. It is as if you were a camera shooting a long shot.

As we store our picture-memories, we also store the feelings that were associated with them. The moment we wish to tell someone about the pictures—describe them, explain them—whatever emotions we have attached to them are immediately triggered. They may have become muted by time and perspective, but they rush to the surface making themselves known in our faces, bodies, and voices. Before the mouth can shape sound into words, the voice assumes the sound of the feelings. For example, when you see a missed old friend, before your mouth can shape the word "hello," your hand is outstretched and the smile is in place and the sound of your voice is warm. The sight of that familiar face has triggered all the sweet feelings associated with your relationship. Your friend doesn't need to hear you say a word to know that you are glad to see him or her again. You have communicated nonverbally, and your friend has read your behavior.

Research studies make it clear that nonverbal communication is the most powerful communication of all. A study done back in 1972 concluded that only 7 percent of interpersonal communication relies on words, while 55 percent results from facial expressions and 38 percent from the way in which people use their voices.

Research conducted in 1982 at the University of New Hampshire by professors Russell I. Haley, Jack Richardson, and Beth M. Baldwin provides further evidence of this. They investigated body language, gestures, the use of eyes, the distance between people, and even settings, music, dress, and sound effects. The study indicated that nonverbal signs trigger positive as well as negative responses in a viewer. The study concluded that these nonverbal signals communicated more powerfully than facts conveyed through verbal language. The respondents in the study assigned feelings to what they saw. These feelings were triggered because what they saw resembled something in their personal picture file of memories, and the picture and the feeling were glued together.

"One picture is worth ten thousand words" is an old adage. However, many actors are put off or dismayed by the idea that their behavior creates a moving picture that audiences read first and best. Although they will readily agree that acting is behaving, or that acting is living truthfully, they seem to feel disenfranchised by the fact that the word "feeling" is nowhere in the definition. The connection between feeling and behaving eludes them.

As I have said, having feelings isn't enough—they must be communicated. That won't happen unless those feelings make themselves known through behavior that someone else can read. Before hearing you speak a word, your audience will read your eyes, face, and body. They will hear a message in the sound of your voice. You will have already cued them to the emotional content of the thought whose details will be made clear through the words.

If there is anything an actor can trust, it is the ability of the body to turn feelings into behavior. If the actor's instrument—voice and body—is functioning without tension, it becomes the Silly Putty of the mind: The vocal and physical instrument communicates, without conscious meddling, the subtlest shades of feeling, responding to the thoughts, images, and desires of the mind. "When the mind is in overdrive," as Michael Caine says, "the body is headed in the right direction."

TELLING A STORY WITH NURSERY RHYMES

Here's a good place to do our first exercise work. The following is a variation of an exercise created by Sanford Meisner for his professional classes.

Have a group of actors sit in a circle. The leader or teacher should choose one member of the group and take him or her into a private corner of the room. The leader then asks the actor to tell the rest of the group about a real event he or she experienced. For the sake of the exercise, the event should be one with high emotional stakes. One of my favorites is: "Tell us about the most frightening thing that ever happened to you."

Here's the challenge, however: The actor must tell the group about the incident using *only* the words of a nursery rhyme. I usually use "Hickory Dickory Dock." The actor may repeat the nursery rhyme as many times as needed to tell the complete story.

The leader should assign a very bland or illogical nursery rhyme so that its plot or emotions won't involve the storyteller's attention. Knowing the exact words of the rhyme is not important. I have had students use only the first two lines and achieve the desired effect. Remember, the words are not important. The actor's story is. Here are some sample ideas for a story topic:

• The most frightening thing that ever happened to me.

• The day I was married.

• The worst opening night I ever had.

• The day my child was born.

• The most embarrassing thing that ever happened to me.

Notice that all of the subjects listed have high emotional stakes. Even the acting student who is very blocked should experience a result if the story is about a peak emotional event.

Once the actor has selected an event to relate, he or she should sit before the group. He or she should not dramatize the story in any way. The object is to tell the story to the group as if the listeners were seated in the actor's living room. The group's goal is then to try to figure out what the story was about.

When the story is over, the leader can prompt the group with questions: Was this event happening directly to the actor, or was the actor watching it happen to someone else? Was the actor alone in the event, or were there other people present? Was the event taking place indoors, or outside, at night or during the day, less than five years ago, more than five years ago?

The story-telling actor does not answer the individual questions—does not confirm them or deny them in any way—as the leader tries to help the group reach a consensus about the content of the story. Then, the leader summarizes the story to the story-telling actor. The actor lets the group know how close they were to the facts of the real event, fills in the details and, most interestingly, affirms the identification of emotional states.

In one recent class, I asked a young actor to tell us the most frightening thing that ever happened to her using the nursery rhyme "Hickory Dickory Dock." My students discussed what they had seen and heard, and they agreed that the young woman had been alone and that the event was happening directly to her. Although the event happened outdoors, the woman seemed to be confined and unable to move about. The event surprised her, and she was not responsible for what happened in any way. They believed the event swirled around her, out of her control, and that the incident was life-threatening. They also understood that she was physically hurt. To this day, she seemed to tell them, she did not know how she survived. Everyone agreed that she was terrified.

The actual event she had been relating was consistent with all these descriptions. She told us that she had been windsurfing, far from shore. A sudden, heavy wind arose and caused the sail to be torn from her grasp. It fell and hit her in the face. The blow cut her and caused profuse bleeding and a semiconscious state. The seas rose with the wind. She felt that she would never make it back to shore. Hanging on for dear life, she struggled for consciousness and strength in the face of what seemed to be overwhelming odds.

My students were astounded at the many details they had correctly perceived—her confinement on the sailboard, for example, and that she had been outside. They certainly were amazed at the accuracy of their interpretation of her feelings.

That so much can be expressed without words is a marvelous revelation to many actors. In these sessions, many of my students gain for the first time some understanding of the mind-body connection. Previous commentary in their acting classes, such as "Trust it" or "Get out of your head," begin to have concrete meaning. They can trust their voices and bodies to make their feelings known. And maybe if they begin to focus on doing something as simple as telling a story, they can stop thinking about *how* they are doing it, *while* they are doing it.

My students are also surprised at the answer to the question, "When does the communication start?" A few actors usually say, "With the first "Hickory," or "With the first gesture." What the group discovers, however, is that if they watch me talking to the actor in the corner, they can see the moment the actor says "yes" to an event idea. The moment the actor thinks about the event, his or her body and face, and even the tone of the released breath, cues them to the kind of event that is about to be communicated. They know whether the story will be sad, silly, happy, frightening, or filled with grief the minute the actor starts to remember. And how does each actor remember? In pictures.

This simple exercise can be done at home as well. You can choose an appropriately emotional event and, using a nursery rhyme, relate the experience aloud, as if to your friends and family in the living room. Indeed, use your family and friends as an audience if you are brave enough, and if they have the interest and patience.

READING PEOPLE

Besides physical and vocal behavior, we read a person's clothing, jewelry and other decoration, and hair style—all of which embody and communicate meaning. The computer called our brain organizes the information it receives through the senses much the same way that the IBM computer organizes data. It creates a master file named "woman," for example, that contains all the material gathered through the senses that relates and finally provides the meaning of "woman." It then has subdirectories which give more precise names to any variations or extensions of the basic data. A buxom peroxide blonde who wears plunging necklines, very tight skirts, and cheap perfume is definitely in the "woman" file, but the subdirectory would definitely not be "kindergarten teacher." We organize the immense amount of stimuli that we receive all the time according to the meaning we've assigned to the images.

Our culture behaves the same way. In order to communicate, it agrees upon the meaning not only of words but also of images. The choice of blue and white as the colors for the Ivory soap wrapper results from the culture's agreement that they are the colors of purity—the soap's major claim to fame.

The extent to which we agree on the meaning of nonverbal cues takes many actors by surprise. For years I have illustrated this idea in my classes by asking each actor to give me one adjective to describe a specific noun. The noun is *librarian*. As I point to individual actors the descriptions I hear are: prudish, glasses, hair in a bun, dour, unsmiling, tall, thin, over thirty-five, single, high neckline. No one even bothers to say female because everyone has made the assumption that a librarian is female. I'm sure that a short, round, jolly, married, male librarian exists somewhere out there, but we wouldn't guess his profession by looking at him. And he hates the stereotype.

These unspoken cultural agreements create the phenomenon of the stereotype. Actors hate the word. To most of them it represents everything they think of as negative in casting. It's almost as if the idea were created to make their careers more difficult. But nothing could be further from the truth.

Because we know that the creation of stereotypes is a function of our cultural experience and is one way we attempt to order that experience, we should allow ourselves to embrace and use them for our benefit. The first benefit is fast communication. In the twenty-eight-second commercial story, the audience needs to know who you are right away. If I'm going to audition for a librarian this afternoon, you had better believe I'll bring my glasses and combs to pin up my hair. I'll probably choose a dress that can be buttoned up tightly as well. My job will be to embellish that easily recognized picture with believable behavior suitable to the story. In commercials, I am what I look like. What may be news to some actors is that this tenet is true in film, television, and theater as well.

Three Common Commercial Stereotypes. *These characters have a few specific features that define them. It should be simple to guess what each does for a living.*

The second benefit that actors can gain from understanding and embracing stereotypes affects the whole issue of headshots and personal presentation. If the general public responds along stereotypical lines, why should agents be any different? They need to know what category of character you fit. Are you a nice young dad, an upscale businesswoman, a Midwest mom, a blue-collar guy, or a Yuppie? You need to make objective decisions about yourself. Not how you would like to be perceived and cast, but how you are perceived and are most likely to be cast. Not everyone is a leading lady or the Everyman who lives next door.

One of the plusses of getting on-camera training is that it gives you an opportunity to see, evaluate, and come to terms with yourself and what you do well. Then you can set about marketing your strengths and clarifying the impression you wish to create. The more specific you are in communicating this information to an agent, the better chance you have of getting a positive response.

Summing up the ideas that will shape the way we communicate our feelings to an audience:

• Seeing is believing.

• What is seen communicates most effectively.

• We attach meaning to what we see.

• The sound or tone of the voice communicates meaning as well.

• Physical and vocal *behavior* communicates.

4

Acting Is Behaving

To act is to do.
      UTA HAGEN

I remember my first New York acting class extremely well. I had been fortunate enough to be accepted as a student by the highly respected teacher and director Wynn Handman. The class met in a studio on West 54th Street, just east of Seventh Avenue, and up several flights of stairs. It was grungy and wonderful. One of the details about that studio that I still remember was the sign that said, "Acting is doing, acting is simple." My thought at the time was: "Easy for him to say!"

Sanford Meisner's statement—that it takes twenty years to make an actor—seemed more sensible. That sounded like work. However, it never occurred to me that Meisner did not necessarily mean twenty years of angst and sweat. With my Judeo-Christian upbringing, I could understand "work." Work is hard. So initially, I had a lot of trouble with Wynn's description of acting as "simple"; simple implied easy—and anything easy was definitely suspect. I have discovered that my feelings were not unique.

The truth of the statement on Wynn's wall seems to be difficult for many young actors to grasp. The energy that performers invest in keeping the process complicated and hard is amazing. I have often thought that by keeping the process "hard work," actors justify their pleasure in doing it. I know I did. And it took a good, long time for that idea to change.

Auditioning and acting in commercials changed it for me. Speed and the camera made it change. Speed meant that there was no time to indulge myself. There was the copy, and I just had to do it. My character, if there was one, had no biography. Truth be told, there was no character! There was no time to delve into my psyche for the appropriate sense memory or emotional preparation. There seemed to be no time for anything.

Mostly, there was no place to hide: no character, no costume, no makeup, and no big baroque emotional life. The commercial's copywriter certainly didn't give me any clues about my character's life before the words and didn't imply a life after them. Consequently, my focus was totally directed toward saying the words. I battled to bend them to my will. It was me against them. It was hard. It was wrong.

Perhaps it was the anxiety attacks that made me back off and rethink what I was doing. Perhaps it was the introduction of the camera into the audition and the disappearance of an audience. Perhaps it was both. Even though I was booking work, the frustration of not understanding why it worked, when it worked, was unnerving. Every audition felt like Russian Roulette. When the camera was introduced into the audition, it took away the last shred of comfort: the familiar feeling of performing for real live people. In the early days, the audition for a commercial was the same as the audition for the theater. You went into a room and all the decision-makers were present. You could get a sense of whether they liked your work or not. They talked to you and gave you their adjustments. Callbacks seldom happened. There was no need for them. Of necessity, the number of actors at the first audition was also very much smaller. You couldn't tie up a full day of the creative team's time and, besides, they couldn't remember that many performances accurately.

The camera changed all that. Now the creatives could view the duplicated audition tape anywhere and anytime they could find a VCR. The need for their presence at the initial casting session was gone. The casting director could tape as many people as the director felt necessary. Now casting sessions could have larger numbers of actors to chose from and the callback became common practice. That was when the director showed up. It was the first time the actors who made the first cut got a chance to work with him. At this point they got feedback and adjustments. More importantly, who they were as *people* had some impact upon the process.

In order to get to the all-important callback, I had to make an impression on the first taped audition. That was the hard one—just me and the camera. What was I going to do that would make the difference and get me called back to work with the director? The casting directors only made things harder for me by telling me to "just be myself." Hadn't I become an actress in order to be other people? Hyperventilating every inch of the way, I resigned myself. I would just do it. I wouldn't "perform" it, just simply do it.

Do what? Not a lot happens in a commercial. There are no complicated plots or car chases, and there are rarely grand passions to tear to tatters. Maybe you talk to a scene partner about back pain. Maybe you talk to the camera about insurance. Maybe you just look at a dinner table and smile.

DOING, NOT ACTING

Commercials required me "to do" simple things. I needed to look and see and respond, make statements, ask questions, drink a cup of coffee. Not pretend to do them, but really do them. Focusing on doing such seemingly mundane activities proved difficult. It didn't feel dramatic or interesting or "enough."

But I learned something. I finally got it. I figured out what Wynn and Meisner had been striving to teach me. I learned that when I completely committed myself to doing each task, it pinned me in the moment. What the camera saw was that no matter how simple the doing, if I was committed to it, I was not only in the moment, but I was appropriately energized. Even more surprising, it was enough.

What was it that committed me and energized me? What was I really doing? I realized that when things were really cooking, my mind was absorbed with what Uta Hagen might call "real thinking": It was evaluating, questioning, investigating, or planning.

In the "look at the dinner table and smile" spot, I discovered that before looking and smiling, during looking and smiling, and even after, my mind was focused. It was focused and occupied with thoughts. These thoughts became the language of an inner monologue. The monologue might go something like this: "What a surprise! How lovely the flowers are! Did Jean remember the napkins? Everything is perfect." One little thought at a time. The thoughts and the ensuing behavior were interdependent. These were not the random, fleeting thoughts of our ordinary existence. They were thoughts I chose to have. The thoughts provoked behavior. Looking at the dinner table and smiling were no longer physical moves that suggested a mood or ambience—they now appeared to come from some real source and were executed as if they were the logical outgrowth of a larger event.

The implications of this idea were mind-boggling. It meant that once I knew what the desired result was, I could devise a series of thoughts that would produce it. I could script my inner monologue! If I could stay focused on my thoughts, I could trust my face, body, and voice to express them. If my mind was "in gear" and doing something, my eyes were never dead.

The famous acting teacher Lee Strasberg said it this way: "When an actor starts to think, life starts." Amazing! And so simple! Thinking was the seminal "doing" for everyone, but most particularly for the actor working in front of the camera.

THINKING AS DOING

When I met my friend David Schramm, he was working consistently in the theater. He is such a wonderful actor that I call him an actor's actor. He graduated from Juilliard, worked as a member of the prestigious Acting Company, and played enough Shakespeare to qualify for a knighthood. Finally, Hollywood beckoned, and David found himself on a sitcom called *Wings*. Having paid his dues in the theater, Hollywood would now pay him in dollars appropriate to his magnificent talent.

I called David in Los Angeles and invited him to fly into New York to teach a workshop in acting on film. After we talked and laughed, he agreed to come. Then he said to me, almost apologetically, "But Joan, all I discovered is that it's all about thinking. Just thinking!" The camera had revealed to David something that he had always known, if not consciously recognized.

The idea of thinking as doing has profoundly influenced the film actor. The great Lillian Gish was quoted as saying:

The camera teaches you what not to do. I used to hang a mirror on the side of the camera, because at first I was making faces. And then I found that you should start with the curtain down, your face in repose, and then whatever you had in mind, you thought it and the camera got it. If you were caught acting, they didn't believe it.

And Bette Davis was quoted as saying: "Talk softly, think loudly."

Because commercials are little scripts that are auditioned and shot in a filmic way—employing a one-camera technique—thinking as doing is a fundamental concept. However, this concept is very different from the idea and critique of "being in your head." I have come to realize that this critique gets in the way of understanding thinking as doing, or *active listening,* or *silent dialogue,* as Shurtleff might call it. Beginning actors hear this critique a lot, and they know it has something to do with thinking, but they are not always sure quite what.

To me, "being in your head" means being aware of yourself and what you are doing while you are doing it. You are focused on you. But thinking as an action is provoked and connected to what is going on *outside* of you. You are focused on someone or some object or activity that is external.

Thinking as an action is part of the communication circle. It is the kind of thinking that occurs when the teacher asks you a question and you then have to think before you can answer. The teacher's question provokes the *doing* of thinking. The action of thinking focuses mental energy. Once you begin thinking, you are energized. And your desire to answer or—not to answer— provokes behavior.

My own experiences and those of others have shown me that this simple idea can be the source of solutions for many problems that confront theatrically trained actors in commercials, as well as performance problems in other venues. In my own work, it made me be specific; made me pay attention to what made the words *happen;* and stopped me from being outside of what I was doing. It made me become the prime mover in the moment of doing it.

There is a wonderful story that is attributed to an experience of Sanford Meisner's. Several actors were working on a scene that began with them waiting for news in a police detention center. The opening section of the scene didn't have any urgency or interest, so Meisner told one actor to walk around the room, silently count the lightbulbs, and at every fourth one give a sigh. He told another actor to study the floor and quietly moan when he found a crack that was a straight line. The third actor was given a similar task. Suddenly that part of the scene was filled with energy, behavior, and tension. Meisner had made them do something. They were thinking: counting, evaluating, judging, and looking. Active thinking replaced passivity with purpose.

I often use the following exercise to illustrate how the camera perceives thinking as active: I put an actor in front of the camera and ask him or her to *silently* do the multiplication table for eight from one to twenty. Then I ask the rest of the class to describe what they see. They always say they see someone doing something. Not only is the actor alive, but he or she is doing something interesting. Most likely, the behavior will be described as "trying to solve a problem."

Wynn Handman was right after all. It is all rather simple:

- Acting is behaving.
- Acting is doing.
- Doing is behaving.
- Thinking is doing.

5

Acting Technique: Lean and Mean

Hold on to the foundation of your technique.
SANFORD MEISNER

It seems to me that the actor-training establishment has become very invested in complicating the process of acting. I don't mean that it goes about confusing actors on purpose. But like any profession, it has its philosophic differences and murky jargon. Words such as "Method," "truth," and "organic" pepper the vocabulary of the actors who come to me. When I ask them what they mean by those words and ideas, they are often at a loss to be specific. Although they have a lot to say, all of it is general. Something is "truthful" because they feel it; the feeling is "organic" because it is real; and it is real because they feel it. Everything is about feeling their feelings. Their exploration of an inner life seems to have shut down their ability to connect to—or even consider—the outside world. Actors feel they have been trained in the Method simply because Konstantin Stanislavsky's name has been invoked. They seldom realize that every major acting teacher of the late twentieth century in America finds the roots of his or her teaching philosophy in the Stanislavsky System.

When I sit and talk with my students, I discover that scene classes have dominated their training. Their training in technique, if there was any, seems to have focused on things like sense memory and personal emotional recall exercises. Stripping away their "emotional covers" is another activity that seems to have taken up a great deal of their time and energy. Getting rid of inhibitions is another exercise that has occupied class time. The psychobabble I hear truly alarms me.

I also find that, very early in many training situations, student actors are assigned scenes that are five or six minutes in length. All too often they are from Chekhov or Shakespeare. Any technique they may have learned rarely makes it into their scene work. Overwhelmed by so many words, these actors are drowned in dramatic material far beyond their reach. If they are lucky, they will be given short, naturalistic scenes in which their focus can remain on a commitment to an action and on active listening, thus providing a bridge for integrating technique and text. But these steps are often missing. As a result, technique remains in one corner and text in another, and the twain never meet.

Worse, evaluations of exercise scenes are discussed in terms of the actor's inability to express truth, be organic, or be in the moment. The comments are expressed in the jargon of each instructor's acting philosophy. But the comments will only be effective if the actors understand what is meant by that jargon. Afterward, they must try to execute their teachers' verbal prescriptions. If the actors are lucky, they will have an opportunity to work again immediately, test out what they thought they understood, and be able to feel a difference in the second go-round. Here "feel" is the operative word, because that is really the only way actors know for themselves that a change in approach has been effective. Working in a new way will feel different from the previous approach. For actors, hearing about how they have changed isn't nearly as good as feeling and, therefore, knowing it for themselves. (And let me stress that that *feeling* is not necessarily a comfortable one.) Should they succeed in changing what they were doing into something that communicates more clearly, they may have learned a piece of usable technique.

In most cases, they have learned something that applies only to that one particular scene. Rare is the instructor who is able to pinpoint an actor's underlying problem or tell the actor how to fix it. The most frequent comments heard in acting classes—"get off the words," "stop thinking so much," or "you're anticipating"—are all about flaws in basic acting technique. But until actors know what to "get onto," or what kind of "thinking" is meant, or how their "anticipating" was revealed, there is little likelihood that their technique will improve.

What is more distressing are actors who have received lessons and exercises in relaxation, in commitment to an activity, or in active listening, but rarely, if ever, apply this knowledge to either the text or their ability to have a believable life on camera.

THE CAMERA AS TEACHER

The camera offers actors a great gift. For the first time they can see exactly what they are doing. No longer do they need to depend on someone else to describe what they are doing or not doing. In front of a camera, flaws in basic technique make themselves blatantly visible. For example, anything that produces visible tension or interferes with concentration will be seen in a flash. Couple that kind of close-up evaluation with the shortness of the story that has to be told in a television commercial, and you have a recipe for getting down to the guts of why performances succeed or fail. There is nowhere to hide.

The camera is honest. Actors no longer have to figure out what the teacher's critique really meant. Their understanding of their performance isn't entirely filtered through someone else's eyes, ears, and mind; they can see and hear for themselves. They will observe the result of everything they are

Feeling is not an acting characteristic

doing consciously and unconsciously. As scary as that sounds, the camera offers actors tremendous rewards. As an actor, seeing the consequences of your approach to your work will either give you courage to continue in the same direction, or convince you that changes need to be made.

FOUR BASIC ACTING SKILLS

The stories that we as actors are asked to bring to life in commercials are, generally speaking, naturalistic ones that rely on our ability to communicate simply and believably. This requires the application of basic acting skills, the foundation of any actor's future development, whether in film or theater.

Learning to work in the compressed film texts that we call TV commercials is a wonderful way both to test the foundations of your acting technique and to begin to adapt that technique to the demands of screen work. If there are any cracks in your foundation, the camera will help you find them, and then you can start the repair work. If you have never had technique training, commercials are a good place to acquire it, because the camera will keep you honest. All this assumes that you are not working in a hold-up-the-product-and-smile commercial class.

Actors require basic skills that fall into four categories: the ability to relax; the ability to concentrate; the ability to listen and respond; and the ability to physicalize. These are learnable skills that allow actors to think, do, and communicate. Notice that there is no category called "the ability to feel."

Relaxation

The ability to release tension and relax gives you access to your mind and body. If the audition and/or performance puts you in a flight-or-fight panic, you will have too much adrenaline in your system to think clearly and, therefore, concentrate. If your physical instrument is tight, it will not be able to resonate with, and thereby communicate, your mind's needs and desires.

Getting control of your physical instrument through release and relaxation is absolutely essential. If you don't treat your body as your primary acting partner, it has the potential to become your acting enemy. Releasing tension and achieving a relaxed and available body can be attained in a number of techniques, and actors may use a number of them during the course of a career.

The breathing techniques that are taught in good vocal production classes are a wonderful way of dealing with tension. A vocal production class is not a singing class. And do not assume that, if you are a singer, you know how to breathe when you walk, sit, stand, or talk. All too often, singers do not possess these skills.

Controlled deep breathing is another way to reduce tension. The mind does not perceive itself to be in danger when your breathing is deep, slow, and steady. Various meditation and stress reduction techniques teach how this breathing is achieved. If you have had good training in relaxation exercises, use them!

If you are in New York City, go to the Actor's Movement Studio. Its founder, Lloyd Williamson, has created a system for working on movement that helps actors release tension and find access to their bodies. His work also guides the actor toward integrating the body, the voice, and the text. He has done wonders for many actors of my acquaintance.

There are many other methods available. The Alexander Technique is another way of fine-tuning and balancing your physical instrument. Or try visualization exercises. They are another route to relaxation. Yoga is a centuries-old technique whose long-term benefits should not be overlooked.

The method is not as important as the result—a responsive, alert, and centered body.

Concentration

Concentration is a life skill that should be taught to everyone in elementary school, for it's a requirement for success in all fields of endeavor.

Too often, the actor's ability to harness mental energy in the pursuit of a single task is not as good as it should be. Good concentration is what allows actors to focus their minds and, therefore, their energy in pursuit of a task. In acting, your commitment to a task means giving it your complete concentration. You can't allow your focus to be pulled to the words, yourself, or to an audience.

Many actors today are too easily distracted. Their power of concentration is weak. There is no doubt that our culture, which prides itself on instant gratification, has contributed to this phenomenon. Whether it's fueled by a fondness for television remote-control buttons or too many preservatives in junk food, actors are not immune from such contemporary concentration-destroyers. Anything that improves and exercises your concentration is helpful. Playing bridge or tennis, doing crossword puzzles, or learning how to tap-dance all qualify as activities that demand concentration. I particularly like those that involve the body and the mind together.

In the beginning, concentration is not always comfortable, particularly if you are not used to it. It is work—maybe the hardest work of all the basic skills. Concentration requires discipline. It is the first lesson in commitment.

Listening and Responding

To listen and respond is to communicate. It is the glue of every relationship, on screen and off. Active listening requires the preceding skill, concentration. When your focus is on yourself or the words, you can't listen.

If you are fortunate enough to be enrolled in classes or programs that employ Sanford Meisner's training techniques, you'll find that listening and response exercises are fundamental in his approach. The basic repetition exercises strengthen concentration and focus. Developed out of his work in the theater, his approach works wonderfully for film acting.

By training actors in the "reality of doing," Meisner's technique creates an awareness of and connection to the world around them. His approach keeps actors responsive and in the moment by training them to be focused on their partners and not on themselves.

Many of the finest film actors have been students of Meisner. Although untutored in his technique, Michael Caine echoes something you might hear from Meisner himself when he says that the best advice he can give "someone who wants to act in movies" consists of three words: "Listen and react."

Physicalization

The ability to communicate physically is crucial to the art of performance. The mind makes itself known through the body. The mind and the body are partners in communication. You can't have one without the other. Actors need them to work as a team. They also need to know how they trigger each other.

Recently, acting teachers have begun to recognize the value of improvisation as a training tool. For years, most of us have enjoyed it only as a performance style. Improvisation makes actors concentrate so that they can hear and respond quickly and appropriately. It also trains actors to physicalize.

Viola Spolin, whose books on improvisation have influenced generations, says, "An actor can dissect, analyze, intellectualize, or develop a case history for a part, but if he is unable to assimilate it and communicate it physically, it is useless." Once again, we have returned to the definition of acting as behavior that communicates.

To prove the validity of this oft-repeated dictum, here's an exercise that my improv faculty members use when teaching skills for commercials. Named "The Macy's Information Booth Exercise" or "Five Through the Door," it really reinforces the idea that if the audience doesn't see it, they won't get it.

The instructor plays the Macy's information clerk by standing behind the camera as if it were the department store's information booth. Each actor's assignment is to enter the frame and ask for the location of a specific item, such as shower curtains. The actor gets the information and leaves but must immediately reenter, without any time lapsing, and ask for the same item again. The actor must enter and leave five times consecutively, each time asking for the same item but *in a different emotional state*—panicked, grieving, irate, embarrassed, and so on. The actor must shift gears in the time it takes to get out and turn around.

When each actor has completed five entrances, the instructor rewinds the tape and plays back what the actors did without playing the sound. Most of the time, the class will be astounded at how little they used their bodies. If they don't physicalize, the result will be little difference in the actors' behavior from entrance to entrance. Consequently, the class won't identify what emotional states each actor was trying to communicate. Repeating the exercise and making the actors use their bodies to quickly make the audience "get it" is a revelation.

Improvisation exercises work wonders for all actors, but particularly actors in commercials, and offer practice in all the basic skills. Moreover, they are a

Theatre Games (handwritten in left margin)

lot of fun. Improvisation exercises remind you that there is a strong element of play in acting. It helps you "make believe." You are doing things *as if* you were in a different state of being or were someone or something else. Your imagination stretches as it is challenged.

It always surprises students to see how fast their minds and bodies can create. Improvisation rewards actors by improving their ability to *quickly* turn ideas into concrete physical and vocal behavior. It offers a way to practice working fast, a crucial skill if you want to succeed in commercial work. And because it all has to happen "right now," it requires courage. Improvisation teaches courage of commitment to an idea.

If there isn't a good commercial class available to you, see if you can find a class in improvisation. There might even be an improv group in your area that you could join. You won't regret it.

USING THE FOUNDATION SKILLS

These four skill categories are the foundation of all good film acting, and acting in commercials is simply good film acting applied to a very short text. Any training program that places major emphasis on the mastery of these skills and their integration with the text will enlarge their student-actors' opportunities for future employment, particularly in front of the camera.

These foundation skills can be acquired with guidance and practice. Learning them requires that actors be focused on the process rather than on some idea of what they think the result should be. One of the most frustrating problems I have had as a teacher is dealing with actors who are always trying to control the result. They have a picture in their heads of how the finished performance should look and sound. Trying to work this way is a prescription for frustration. You must stay focused on what you are doing right now in the moment—not on the result that you would like to achieve later.

Almost everything that actors in commercials need to have in their tool kit involves the ability to relax, to concentrate, to listen and respond, and to physicalize. How you will apply these techniques to the text becomes the next challenge.

Part Three
COMMERCIAL ACTING TECHNIQUES

6
The Camera

The camera doesn't have to be wooed, it already loves you deeply.

MICHAEL CAINE

Let's talk about camera technique. Remember poor Jane, who didn't have any? She stood in front of that little studio Sony, saw its unyielding metal, plastic, and glass, and froze. She had no idea what lay behind the camera's one big eye or how it saw. Jane and the camera never had been properly introduced to one another.

Notice that I refer to the camera as if it were a person. The first step in acquiring a camera technique is to examine how you think about the camera itself. The camera functions as the audience or your scene partner and will be your constant companion in film and television. Unlike a theater audience, the camera will rarely disappear into the darkness when you begin to act. And as you move from the audition studio to the sound studio, the size and sometimes the number of the cameras increase. The camera is the major force that requires you to change the way you apply your acting skills.

SINGLE VS. MULTIPLE CAMERA TECHNIQUE

Commercials are shot in a film technique—but what does that mean? How does that differ from a television technique? And what implications does it have for actors and the way they work? For our purposes, the number of cameras present at the shoot defines film and television differences.

Single Camera

In film, only one camera is present. That camera will record everything that will be shot, photographing the action from different points of view. The film is then developed and cut and put back together in a way that tells the story in the most effective way—this is the *editing* process. A scene or a section of a scene, called a *set-up*, is generally filmed first in what is called the master shot. The master sees all the action that will happen in that section. That section is shot over and over until the director feels all the values are correct, and then it will be "frozen," in much the same way that we finalize or freeze a performance before the opening of a theater piece. The camera will then film the action from different points of view and different distances—moving in for close-ups, for example, and also assuming the place of an actor in the scene in order to record the scene as that actor would see it. The camera may even record the point of view of *every* actor in the scene. The scene may be shot and reshot a multitude of ways before the director feels sure that all the action is "covered."

This way of working is very new to the actor who has had experience only in the theater, where we tell the story in a linear fashion—meaning that we start at the beginning and move sequentially forward in the action. Once the actor's initial preparation is done and the entrance made, one moment moves logically out of the previous moment and forward into the next moment. Once you have started the performance, you can't go back and start again. Filming is a *nonlinear* process: You are required to replay the same section of the story over and over again, while matching not only the physical moves but matching the emotional colors as well. You have to constantly restart your emotional engine and keep the moment completely spontaneous in appearance, as if it had never happened before. This is a challenge.

There is also the challenge of playing to a camera lens instead of a live scene partner. If the camera is shooting the scene from your partner's point of view, then the big glass lens of the Panaflex camera will replace your partner's face. For the actor without camera training, this can be an unsettling experience.

In film, the sequence of shooting the story always accommodates the set-ups. Locations, weather, studio availability, and a whole host of other production considerations dictate the nonlinear order in which a movie's story will be shot. It is not unusual for the actor to be working on the end of film before the opening. This requires that the arc of a character's development be very clear to the actor before filming starts. You may rehearse a section of a film before it is shot, but you'll rarely rehearse the entire film before shooting begins. Stanislavsky said that the actor in film needed much stronger concentration and technique than the actor in theater since he or she often died before being born. The great man recognized the heightened demands of concentration and preparation that are placed upon the actor in film because of the one-camera technique.

Features, much of episodic television, industrial films, and commercials employ the one-camera approach.

Multiple Cameras

Television relies upon the multiple camera technique, in which there are usually three, and sometimes four, cameras being used simultaneously. Soap operas, or daytime dramas, and sitcoms are done this way. Both of these story forms are shot in a *linear* fashion: Shooting starts at the beginning of the story line and continues through to the end. That can happen because all the cameras, according to a preplanned shot sheet, are videotaping the action. The director, seated in a booth, watches by way of a monitor for each camera. The director thus sees what the cameras are seeing and switches between them and records the shots that work—in effect *editing* the videotape while the action is happening. There is little or no cutting and pasting after the fact.

The good news is that actors get a chance to rehearse before the final taping. (More time is given to rehearsals in sitcoms than in soaps.) However, once taping has begun, actors rarely get a chance to go back and retape a portion of a scene that didn't work. Also good news is that actors do not have to keep a performance fresh time after time. What they must do is give a believable performance while always making sure they hit very specific physical marks that accommodate the cameras and the lights. Physical movement is prescribed and restricted to meet the requirements of the shot sheet that has been prepared prior to the rehearsal and taping.

The set-ups for each day's recording are three to four sets. Individual walls or furniture do not need to be moved in order for the camera to get the shot. Point-of-view shots are accomplished by having the camera shoot over an actor's shoulder to photograph his or her scene partner's responses or dialogue.

As you can see, the single- and multiple-camera mediums pose different challenges. However, one thing does not change, and that is the camera itself. Whatever the camera approach, the communication over *real space* does not change. It is truly the fact that separates camera from theater performance.

COMMUNICATION OVER REAL SPACE

Trained for the theater, most of us have learned what we must do physically and vocally to be seen and heard by an audience. Whether the space was a rehearsal hall or a thousand-seat house, we have been taught to remember that our stage performance must project to the last row. We have struggled with the problem of keeping our work believable within the given dramatic circumstances while projecting it for communication over a larger physical distance. When actors who have a great deal of experience filling theatrical space, whether in a classroom or on a Broadway stage, begin acting in front of a camera, they often continue to project—and their performance is a disaster.

Once a camera has interposed itself between you and your audience, the responsibility for being adequately seen and heard has been lifted from your shoulders. The director, the camera crew, and the sound technicians are responsible for making sure that what needs to be seen and heard is seen and heard. For the film actor, communication over real space is the rule.

Communication over real space is what we do in everyday life. For example: I'm walking down Fifth Avenue and I see my friend, Casey, on the other side of the street. I wave and I shout, "Casey!" My voice is loud and my waving gesture huge. Without conscious planning, my body and my voice adjust themselves to be seen and heard across a busy New York street. Now Casey has seen me and has crossed the street, and we go for coffee. Seated across the table from one another, our voices and gestures are no longer huge. Since we now have to bridge only the three feet between us in order to be understood, our bodies and voices have unconsciously adjusted downward in physical size and vocal projection. They have responded to the distance that the mind perceives between speaker and listener.

Our minds automatically size our communicating behavior, and this unconscious response is a great gift to our film acting technique. If you are in a film scene, and both you and the other characters appear in the frame, your voice and body should automatically size your vocal level and physical gestures for the distance between you and them, while also adjusting to any given circumstances surrounding the action. (Examples of such circumstances might be the sound of rain beating on the roof or the fear of discovery.)

In television, if the camera is shooting your dialogue over your scene partner's shoulder, what matters is the distance between you and your partner. In film, when your partner is replaced by the camera so that we can shoot the scene from his or her point of view, you need to remember what the distance was in the "two-shot" (see illustration, page 50) and match it. Simply by thinking about it, your instrument should size your behavior appropriately.

Framing

In the audition, when you are speaking to the camera as if it were a person, it is the framing that dictates the real space between you and that person. By that I mean how much of you is seen on the monitor dictates how far away the viewer perceives you to be from your unseen partner. If you ask most casting directors in the audition what the framing is, they will tell you. (Asking intelligent questions and making use of the answers is a sign of a professional, so don't be shy.) If you are told that you are in a medium close-up, it means that they have you framed on the monitor from the chest to the top of your head. This shot is the equivalent of having your scene partner stand about three to four feet away from you. The camera, in fact, may be ten to fifteen feet away. However, you must let the framing govern your projection. The rule of thumb is: The less of you there is in the frame, the less distance exists between you and your partner.

Exercise: Sizing Your Projection Needs

To understand the film actor's relationship to real space, try this exercise. Stand in front of a friend, about one foot away. Notice how much of your

Closeup	*Medium closeup*	*Mid-shot*
12 to 18 inches	*2 to 3 feet*	*6 to 8 feet*

Common Camera Shots and Corresponding Distances in Real Space.

SPACE PROJECTION

The Two-Shot and the Single Shot. *In the two-shot (top), the camera frames both you and your scene partner. In the single shot (bottom), the camera shoots your dialogue from your partner's point of view, so you must remember what distance separated you and your partner in the two-shot.*

friend you can see. Now, move backward, two feet at a time. Remain focused on your friend's face. Without moving your head, see how much more of the face and body come into view as you move away. Move backward until you can see your friend from head to foot.

Now repeat this same exercise with one variation. Add the communication "Hi!" with every backward step. You should experience a gradual change in your vocal projection. At some point you may feel the urge to add a gesture. Go with it.

Once you assimilate the concept of on-camera acting as communicating over real space, you should notice powerful results. In my workshops and seminars with beginning actors, this concept produces immediate results. Because it encourages real and familiar behavior, my students' believability increases. It also allows them to start to really do, rather than perform, in front of a camera.

Casting directors often tell actors to "just talk to me like a friend across the kitchen table." I am sure that this note is heard so frequently because of the trained actor's habit of reaching for the back of the house. Actor-singers from musical comedy backgrounds seem to be plagued by this problem. However, they make great actors in commercials once their energies have been focused in real space.

Most importantly, by trusting in the automatic sizing of gesture and sound, you can rid yourself of the idea that acting in film means that you must pull back and be smaller. That idea is dangerous since it contributes to a loss of energy and a constriction of movement—an undesirable result. The concept of real space allows you to maintain your intensity and urgency while trusting your voice and body to communicate in a way that the camera will see as natural and real. The viewer will recognize your work as believable behavior because it will be appropriate to the size of the picture on the screen. It will match viewers' expectations, which are the result of their real-life experiences.

One caution: Everything I have said in this section presupposes that the actor has a fairly unconstricted physical instrument. If the body or voice is blocked, the actor will always strain to get through that tension. That strain, particularly in the voice, might result in overprojection or overarticulation. Easy and natural communication will be hard to achieve until underlying tensions are released.

MY CAMERA, MY FRIEND

The casting director says, "Just talk to me!" The teacher says, "See somebody in the lens." The director says, "Just pretend the camera's not there." Here we are, faced with this mechanical monster that is sometimes less than three feet away, and we're supposed to relax and either talk to it or ignore it completely. How can we do that? I believe we can, by changing the way we think about the camera and by understanding the way it sees us.

I wasn't kidding when I said that Jane's problem was that she hadn't been introduced to the camera. It is imperative that you come to grips with its continuing presence. It is there to stay. Because the camera is your acting companion, I have discovered that it really helps to start the film-acting process by first personalizing the camera in a way that works for you. To personalize it in a productive way, it's necessary to know a little bit more about the way it sees.

The camera will always be watching. As Michael Caine says, its devotion to you is that of a lover: It watches you in blinding detail and adores your behavior, every single nuance of it. It adores you because your behavior lets it know how you feel. The more you show the camera how you feel—good, bad, or indifferent—the more it cares. Like a lover, it looks into your eyes and searches for the answer to the question, "What's going on with you?"

As Shakespeare wrote, "The eyes are the mirror of the soul." The camera shares that belief, and therefore, it cannot be lied to. Best of all, it will not judge you. It loves you unconditionally. The more of your secret self you share with it, the more you can trust it to take care of you.

I began to really understand this idea one summer on a ranch out West. The ranch belonged to the legendary John Wayne, "the Duke," who had been hired to be the first television spokesman for a new headache remedy. I was with the production crew hired to film the spot. Wayne was in his final years and was not in good health. He stayed in his trailer most of the time. When he did emerge to talk to the director or the clients, he was not pleasant or easy to deal with.

I wondered how Wayne was going to get through the job successfully because his face and voice betrayed his personal stress. The crew adjusted and set the lights with the stand-in, who took the Duke's place leaning against the split-rail fence. Then Wayne's prize bull was marched into the pasture in the background, and we crossed our fingers.

Wayne emerged from his trailer and slowly crossed to the fence, expressionless. He leaned on the fence and ran the copy. Then the script supervisor asked him to run the lines for time. He cooperated with a flat voice and an expressionless face. The director cued action, and then it happened: It was as if no person or thing existed for the Duke—except the camera. Everything was shut out. Strain and stress dropped away from him. He seemed to be joined to the lens by a silken thread. He melted into a private relationship with it and in an instant was the John Wayne we all knew—strong, charming, and ever so slightly vulnerable. It was safe for him to be that way with the camera because he knew it loved him. He wasn't so sure about the rest of us. What he knew was that the camera would never use the knowledge of his heart against him. He knew that it was safe to be open and unguarded in front of it.

Like John Wayne, you must personalize the camera in a way that helps you perceive it as understanding and loving. For myself, I imagine that the audition camera is Millicent Martian, the friendly and curious extraterrestrial. All she wants to know is what makes me tick. She loves every little detail of my behavior. I got this idea from the way the camera looks in reality. Mounted on a tripod, she has three legs. Sometimes she puts on her rolling shoes, or wheels, so she can move. Her one arm sticks out of her back, and wires service her life-support system. Her head has one big eye that just wants to watch me, and sometimes her red heart light (the tally light) is shining brightly. She will be anyone I want her to be. The most castable actor I have ever encountered, she loves to play make-believe. She will always look like Millicent to me, but I can treat her as if she were anyone from a killer to a king. She only wants to be invited to play with me. She is my perpetual scene partner, my perpetual playmate, my friend.

THE AUDITION SPACE

The playing space in an audition studio is very different from that of the actual set where you will shoot the finished product. So are the camera and the lighting and sound equipment. Audition rooms can range from a small hotel suite equipped with a camcorder to a good-sized studio with an eight-thousand-dollar video camera. The quality of the lighting equipment is equal to the quality of the camera. Almost without exception, the audition cameras, even the expensive ones, are not able to produce a broadcast-quality picture. Even though they can be larger in size and do more things, audition cameras look very similar to their home-video cousins.

Usually, there is little or no set in the commercial audition. You are asked to sit in a chair or stand on a mark and talk to the camera or play a scene in front of it. The mark is the spot where the lighting converges for the best picture. It is also within the camera's focal length, which is usually thirteen to fifteen feet from lens to subject.

Lighting instruments will vary. Larger and better-equipped studios may have three-point lighting. This means a backlight illuminates your hair and separates you from the back wall, a key light stands out front and slightly to the side, and a fill light on the other side fills in the shadows. The casting director wants even, balanced lighting, without harsh contrasts and shadows. Unfortunately, they don't change the lighting to suit the individual actor. It's a case of "one size fits all."

The needs of the camera and the casting director will always come first. That's not because anyone wants to be mean, but because the speed of the audition and the requirements of the equipment mandate what's possible.

It is best to imagine your playing space in front of the camera as the same as a proscenium stage: There are three walls to what might be a room, and then there is the imaginary "fourth wall" separating the actors' private world on the stage from the audience. In a studio, this fourth wall extends across the face of the camera, and the camera is the audience.

The rules about the fourth wall that we know from Acting 101 apply. You maintain the illusion that you are within a private room with no one watching as long as you do not break that fourth wall. You do break it by making

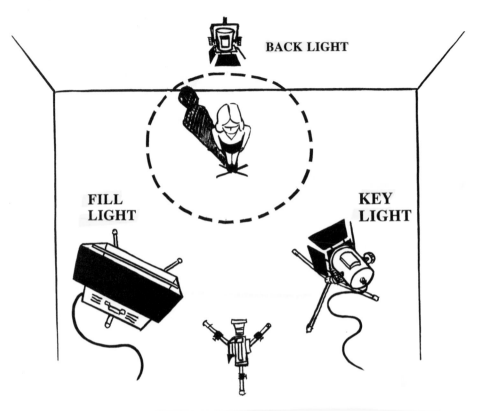

BACK LIGHT

FILL
LIGHT

KEY
LIGHT

Three-Point Lighting. *In this camera setup, the actor stands in a circle of light created by key light, fill light, and back light.*

eye contact with your audience. In your proscenium-stage solitude, the audience becomes an omniscient observer, seeing all without being seen. The same is true in front of the camera. As long as I don't look Millicent in the eye, she will allow me my privacy, and I can pretend she's not there. I can look above the lens, below the lens, and on either side—as long as I don't establish eye contact. Therefore, I can use that imaginary wall, look at it, place a window in it, and hang a picture on it (in my imagination, of course) and still stay private within my "room."

But once you establish eye contact, the camera stops being the audience and is transformed into a person in the scene with you. By looking at it, you give it life.

A significant difference between the proscenium stage and the camera's stage and is the shape of the playing space. Theater stages have depth, front to back, upstage to downstage. They also have width. Most often, they resemble a squarish box. The camera's playing space is long—side to side—and

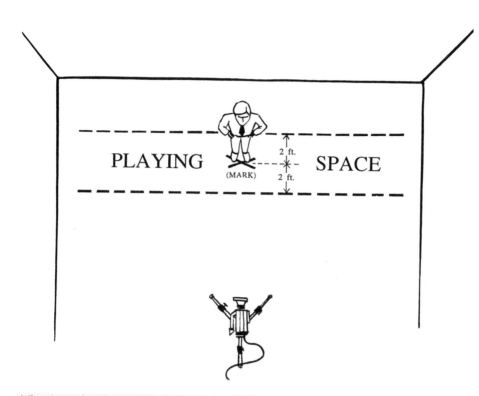

The Actor's Playing Space Before a Camera. *You cannot play too far upstage or too far downstage without being out of the light, in too much light, or, possibly, out of focus.*

narrow in depth. That is the result of the camera's focal length and the fact that in the audition the camera rarely has wheels, so it cannot follow you. It is also the result of the way the lights are focused to converge on one playing space that is the correct distance from the lens. The space is only about four feet wide, extending two feet on either side of the mark, both toward and away from the camera.

Cheating to Stay in Focus

Because the audition camera usually does not have on its rolling shoes and cannot move with you across the stage, it will turn its head as much as possible in order to see your face. But as you move too far right or too far left of its centerline, it loses contact. Since the camera hates to lose your eyes, you have to adjust—or cheat—so that your good relationship with your friend can be preserved.

Cheating is accomplished in front of the camera the same way it is accomplished onstage—by angling the body. The guiding principle for the camera is: If you can't see the camera, even in your peripheral vision, then the camera can't see you.

If you can see the camera out of the side of one eye, then the camera can see enough of your eyes and face to read your thoughts and feelings. In order to guarantee that the lens always has access to your face, make sure that you are never on a ninety-degree angle to the camera. If you are facing your partner in a two-shot, remember the stage rule and keep your downstage foot—the foot nearest the camera—back. The downstage shoulder follows, creating a nice forty-five-degree angle that invites the camera to watch without impediment.

The Right Way to Cheat Toward the Camera. *It is your responsibility to be aware of the adjustments necessary to keep the angle of your body open to the camera's eye. Keep yourself, your face, and your behavior visually available to the camera. This is the etiquette required if you want the camera to remain your friend!*

7

How to Recognize Commercial Forms

Form is the shape or structure of something,
while content is the material being shaped.
FRANCIS HODGE

All commercials are not created equal. They come in different shapes and sizes. They do their job in different ways. The way in which a commercial story is told says something about the message that is trying to be communicated. The more we know about the message—the script we are given to work on—the better equipped we will be to make informed and interesting acting choices.

Learning to read commercial copy with a critical eye is important for the actor who wishes to give good auditions. A large number of actors perceive advertising copy as foreign and phony. Consequently, the very idea that they have to perform it either throws them into panic or calls up their resistance. Even after many actors are told that their job is not to sell the product, but to tell the story, the copy itself still "freaks" them.

The truth is that commercial copy is not always actor-friendly. It may contain syntax unfamiliar to the human tongue. It may include dialogue that does little more than ask questions about the product and then provide answers by listing the product's benefits. The copy may consist of a single line or, worse, it may have no lines.

COPY = SCRIPT

In order to make the most of their skills, actors need to read and understand commercial copy the way they read and understand a film or theater script. One of the things that prevent them from doing this is the name of the material itself—the copy. "Copy" connotes high-powered, high-pressured delivery— it means being a snake-oil salesman.

Actors are much better off once they can think of ad copy as a script, as a text they are preparing for performance. That simple idea allows them to begin the process of *acting* rather than of selling. Scripts are precious to us actors; we take them seriously because we can't do our job without them. Within a script's pages we find the characters we are supposed to bring to life, as well as the information we need to create them. We read a script thoroughly before making any decisions about what we might want to do with the character we are supposed to play. We analyze the script and make acting choices based upon the words and clues the author has provided. Most of us would no sooner pick up an unknown script, open it, and start reading our assigned part aloud than we would jump off a building. Yes, there are such things as "cold readings," but even in these situations we usually have a chance to read through the script or audition scene a least once—any reading with less preparation would be positively arctic.

Nevertheless, you would be surprised how many actors pick up a piece of commercial copy and start saying the lines out loud as they read through it the first time. In order to get the most out of commercial auditions, you must start by valuing the material you have to work with and taking it seriously.

You must be aware by now that a concept for an advertising campaign doesn't just happen overnight. Neither does the script for the campaign's commercials. Every word has been thoroughly discussed and debated and carefully honed to deliver the most impact in the least amount of time. This doesn't guarantee that the end product will be good. Just like plays, there are well-conceived and well-written commercials and ones that are awful. Over the course of your career, you'll audition for and perform in more poor plays than the good ones. The same holds true for commercials. However, as with plays, a poor script should never be used as an excuse for giving an ill-conceived or badly executed audition or performance. Your job, in many instances, will be to make a silk purse out of a sow's ear.

The ultimate quality of a commercial is not the performer's concern. As an actor, your job is to make the audition script work. The better you can do that, the more chance you have of booking the job, even though your ability to make the script work during the actual shoot will depend not only on the material but on the contributions of the people who surround you.

Make no mistake, the more you dismiss the commercial script as "just a commercial" or moan about the fact that "people don't talk this way," the more you commit audition suicide. Your attitude matters. Approach commercial copy in the same craftsmanlike way you would a play. That kind of thoughtful attention will reveal reams of information that you'll need in order to audition well.

Your first order of business is to treat commercial copy with respect, as the offspring of serious creative endeavor. Again, because of the time constraints not a word or action is wasted; even the choice of how to tell the story is important to the message. Every creative decision has been made to support the overall objective, so the more you understand the structure, style, language, and logic of these advertising stories, the more you will be able to apply your acting technique with success.

FORM: THE STRUCTURE OF THE STORY

Boy meets girl, boy gets girl, boy loses girl—it's a story older than *Romeo and Juliet*. Even so, this story has been used in many different performance genres or forms. The plot of *Romeo and Juliet,* for example, has served as the basis for a play, a ballet, a musical play, and a film. The way the story has been told has changed in each of these—not the story itself. The way a story is told is what I call its *form*.

Commercial stories are written in different performance forms. Here is a simple story that could be told in several different forms:

```
I get jangled nerves from drinking regular coffee.
I discovered Calm decaffeinated coffee.
I drink Calm and I stay calm.
```

If I were an advertising copywriter, I could dramatize this commercial story using one of three common forms:

1. I could dramatize this story using slice-of-life scenes that involved two or more characters.

    In the first scene, a woman tells her boss how she messed up at a meeting because she was too "wired" on caffeine. The boss offers her a cup of Calm. A week later, the woman is at the head of a conference table giving a terrific presentation. Then she leans over and thanks her boss for introducing her to Calm.

2. I could write the story as a monologue that the character shares with the camera.

    The character would sit at her kitchen table and tell you how her job as a high school teacher was highly stressful. She'd tell you how glad she was to be able to have a delicious cup of Calm in the morning. "In my job," she'd confide, "I can't afford to drink a coffee that's going to make a hard job harder."

3. I could write a story in which the actors don't speak at all.

    I'd just show—without words—the bad results from not drinking Calm contrasted with the good results from drinking it. I would use only visuals of the actors and their behavior. An off-camera voice might ask, "Had too much coffee this morning?" The visual might show an anxious-looking executive seated in a meeting drumming his fingers and tapping his foot. The boss notices and looks at him disapprovingly. The off-camera voice says, "Why don't you try Calm? The decaffeinated coffee." The next visual is of another executive seated in the same meeting and looking attentive and composed. The boss notices and has a favorable reaction.

Most commercial scripts take one of these three forms. Madison Avenue has devised clever and very appropriate names for each one, and I have devoted a chapter to each—slice-of-life, spokesperson, and MOS.

Scene Format = Slice-of-Life

Commercials that use the scene format take the so-called *slice-of-life* approach. Like Example 1 above, they aim to give viewers the feeling that they are peeking into someone's window and seeing just a moment in the character's ongoing life story. Conceptually, this is no different from a scene prepared for an acting class and, as you'll see, a lot of the acting preparation is similar. Many times, writers choose the slice-of-life form when they wish to imply or underscore ideas about the product through characters and their relationships. Generally, these are emotional ideas about the product rather than facts about it. Relationships in these commercial scripts are always stereotypical.

> *Slice-of-Life Scene*
> Daughter (looking through a scrapbook): Mom, what was my first word?
> Mother: It was . . . "Daddy."
> Daughter: Well, my second word must have been "Mom."
> Mother (serving coffee): Actually, I think it was "chocolate."
> Daughter (laughs): Figures. (She drinks coffee and enjoys it)
> Mother: Some things never change . . .
> Voice-over: Double Mocha Chocolate. The incredibly chocolate coffee, new from Trademark Coffees.
> Daughter (indicates product): Can I take this back to my apartment?
> Mother: Sure . . . as long as you take all your old books and scrapbooks and. . . .
> Voice-over: Double Mocha Chocolate. One of three great chocolate flavors from Trademark Coffees.

The mother–daughter relationship in this sample script is stereotypical. The good mother cares deeply for her grown daughter and shows her affection by remembering that as a child her daughter always loved chocolate. Because the daughter is so special to her, the mother treats her as a special guest by serving a special coffee. We could sum up the message of this spot by saying, "Serving Trademark Coffee shows how caring you are and how special you think your family and guests are."

Monologue Format = Spokesperson

The monologue format employs spokesperson copy. It means that there is one person on camera, and that person is talking either *to* or *with* the camera.

The prepositions "to" and "with" are crucial considerations for the actor. They indicate a real difference in the primary goal of the writer.

The spokesperson script that talks *to* the audience is designed to clearly communicate information to the ear of the listener. It is the kind of writing that we find in industrial films and narration. The actor's primary goal is to make sense of this presentational material. Considerations of emotional tone are secondary to communicating the facts in an intelligent way. This kind of material demands that the actor have a good sense of language, because in auditions the actor will be asked to make this form of commercial sound easy and conversational in its delivery.

The monologue format is easily recognizable by looking at the pronouns: "You" and "your" dominate it. The script is about the listener. The spokesperson remains unidentified, and could be of either sex—I've nicknamed this spokesperson form the "androgynous spokes."

Androgynous Spokes Monologue to *the Camera*
```
Acid indigestion sufferers: All antacids are not
    alike.
Di-Aid is different. It's both antacid and anti-
    gas.
Look.
These mixtures illustrate the misery of acid
    indigestion when complicated by gas.
Compare a plain antacid to Di-Aid.
See, plain antacids are not made to relieve this
    problem.
But the Di-Aid difference gives fast relief from
    excess acid and fast relief from gas.
Compare for yourself.
Get the Di-Aid difference.
```

The spokesperson copy that talks *with* the audience is equally easy to identify. Here the operative pronouns are in the first person: "I, me," and "mine." Who is speaking and how he or she feels are as important, if not more important, than the facts that may be mentioned about the product. I've nicknamed this kind of monologue "character spokes." Dramatic in its attempt to engage the audience in an emotional experience, the copy demands the application of good script analysis and acting skills. The form implies that you are talking with someone, which means you might get an answer, as in a conversation. I guarantee that the direction most often given to actors in the audition studio is, "Be real and conversational." Since this is the kind of spokesperson copy that most actors will encounter in an audition, don't wait to be told to be real and conversational. Once you see those pronouns, you should know what they want.

Character Spokesperson Monologue with *the Camera*

```
Well, who ever said football was the cleanest
    game in the world?
But this team of mine, and their Daddy, must get
    extra points for dirty clothes.
Just look! Mud and dirt from head to toe—
    perspirey, too.
What fantastic luck that I found Cleans with
    natural cleansing ingredients.
Cleans gets everything a new kind of clean you
    want to get close to.
```

Unlike the unidentified spokesperson who speaks *to* the camera, in this monologue the speaker is a real person—a mother. Her emotional tone is as important as the facts that made her feel that way. She feels lucky to have found the product, and as a result she has no laundry problems. Her feelings are as vital to the success of the message as the fact that the product contains "natural cleansing ingredients."

Script Without Dialogue = MOS

The script that has no dialogue is called MOS, an acronym that stands for "minus optical strip." Technically, the term means that the picture will be shot without simultaneously recording any sound. The soundtrack will be added later. (Within the industry, there is a more romantic explanation for the term. In the early days of talking pictures, there were several well-known German directors working in Hollywood. When they spoke English, they had difficulty pronouncing the letter "W." So when they said, "We will shoot this scene without sound," it often sounded like, "Ve vill shoot this scene mittout sound." Therefore, MOS.)

These scripts most closely resemble improvisations. In the majority of MOS auditions, actors don't get any information about the content of the script until they are in the room with the casting director. Then they are told whatever they need to know in order to create the scene. That is why these auditions can make you feel like one of those improvisation performers who takes ideas and suggestions from the audience and immediately uses them in a comedy sketch. However, MOS commercials are not always comedic.

In most MOS auditions, there is no time to prepare. Your skills have to be razor-sharp, and you must be able to create right in the moment. Here is a sample MOS advertisement for a brand of film.

MOS Script

```
A young grandmother and grandfather are seated
outdoors at a family picnic. In front of them is
their four-year-old grandson. Grandpa has a
camera, and Grandma tries to get the boy to pose
```

and look at the camera so Grandpa can take a
picture. They succeed and have a warm moment
with each other as they watch their grandson
return to his play.

Agents love to send beginners to this kind of audition. They think they are
easy because there are no lines. My experience is that these are the commercial auditions that drive actors crazy. Most actors feel lost at sea, thrown over-
board by the speed at which they are expected to invent. Speaking lines of
dialogue seems more familiar, even if they are commercial lines.

OTHER COMMERCIAL FORMS

The slice-of-life, the spokesperson, and the MOS are the three major forms of
commercial copy that actors will encounter in auditions, but there are other
formats. They tend to evolve from popular forms of entertainment. Music
video, for example, which spawned entire cable television channels, has led
advertisers to create commercials that imitate them. Dancers and musicians,
rather than actors, are most in demand for these.

The prime-time program *Candid Camera* increased the popularity of the
hidden-camera spot. "Real people" interviews, sometimes called "testimonials"
seem to be returning, perhaps because of viewer fascination with talk shows.
Animated spots are increasingly popular and cash in on our love of cartoon
characters.

It is only natural that advertisers follow popular trends in entertainment.
Doing so allows them to communicate ideas about a product simply by telling
their advertising story in a specific way that exploits viewers' current tastes.
Employing trendy forms helps them reach a specific segment of the buying
public. Look at the products that employ the mock music video; they aim at a
buying audience between the ages of thirteen and twenty-two. Soft drinks frequently use this form to sell their products. Wine advertisers, on the other
hand—because their product is more expensive and requires a more educated
taste—tell their stories in scenes which stress special feelings, special events,
special relationships, and the acquisition of a higher status among a group of
loving friends. Their market is a generally older, more mainstream group that
has more money to spend.

In my thirty years of experience performing in this medium, I have seen
the popularity of faddish forms rise and recede with the tide of public taste.
However, over the same period the slice-of-life, the spokesperson, and the
MOS have remained in constant use. They are the forms that will occupy our
investigation in the coming chapters.

DOING YOUR HOMEWORK

Identifying the way a commercial script is formatted is the first step in analyzing it. Probably the best way to practice identifying the different forms adver-

tisers use is to turn on the television and watch them. If you are seriously interested in working in commercials, study them. From now on, if you want to get a snack or switch channels while viewing, do so during the regular programming. Pay attention during the commercial breaks.

As you practice identifying the form of a television ad, remember that a scene can be very short—just one line for each character. Similarly, a monologue can be abbreviated into one or two lines spoken to the camera. For example, some commercials use vignettes, a series of mini-monologues spoken by a number of actors. These ads are composed of several shots of different people speaking to the camera.

When you're watching a slice-of-life commercial scene, try to identify what it is about the relationship that says something about the product. Remember that the characters' relationships are designed to imply ideas, not facts, about the product. For example, perhaps the commercial scene is implying that the product has stood the test of time but is not old-fashioned. This idea could be reinforced by an attractive working mother telling her teenage daughter about her lifelong beauty soap. It also could be as simple as the idea that honesty exists between good friends and, therefore, one friend's information about a product or service, given with care and concern, is truthful and to be trusted.

Listen carefully to the off-camera voice when you spot an MOS. Think about how the visual story expands upon or illustrates what the voice-over is saying. You will notice that the off-camera voices sometimes speak directly to on-camera actors, whose task is rather like having to react to the voice of God.

Start doing your homework by paying attention to television commercials. There is a lot to learn. A word of caution, however: Watch and evaluate. Do not try to copy what you see on the screen. There is a great deal of difference between what you see in the final version and what booked the job for the actor in the audition. By doing your homework you will complete the basic research necessary to be proficient at analyzing commercial scripts—before you try acting them.

8

Acting Styles in Commercials

Style is what makes form individual and specific.

FRANCIS HODGE

"What do they want?" That question is asked a hundred times a day. Actors ask it of agents, casting directors, and other actors. Almost every auditioning actor feels that if he or she had some idea of what "they"—the ad agency's client—wanted, the actor might have a shot at giving it to them and getting the job. At times, actors will hear someone offhandedly answer, "They don't know what they want." While that may be true to some extent (they can't know exactly whom they'll eventually cast), the real answer is simpler: "They" want a performance that makes the script work.

No one can make a script work except an actor. The best compliment that was ever paid to me inside the audition room was, "If anyone can make this work, you can." Casting directors may or may not be much help. Most often they will simply reiterate the commercial story that you had just read before you walked in. Furthermore, their comments during the audition— "be bigger," "have more fun with it," "be more real"—won't necessarily clarify the specific demands of the material.

I have always felt the need to find more reliable methods of dealing with commercial scripts and auditions. As I discussed in the previous chapter, form was the first way I began to organize and analyze the material I encountered while auditioning. However, it became clear to me that each form required different performance considerations (each of which will be explored in depth later on). What also became clear was that there were different strategies for communicating the client's message within those forms. Scenes were scenes, for example, but the way the scenes were written varied. If I could identify how they were attempting to reach their audience, I might have a way of knowing more about what the material required in order to make it work. Knowing more about the logic of the writing would help me get to the logic of the playing. It would help me to better prepare outside the audition room. At this point, I began to formulate my ideas about style.

COMMERCIAL STYLES

Plays differ in their style, and so do commercials. The Shakespearean comedy, the Molière comedy, and the Neil Simon comedy are all plays and all comedies, yet they are very different. All deal with the universals of the human experience, but they present their characters and characters' experiences in language and circumstances that their contemporary audiences would have recognized and easily understood. Their plays' thematic messages have been molded by their time. These differences in dramatic conception are one of the first causes of stylistic differences.

Alexander Dean and Lawrence Carra, in *Fundamentals of Play Directing,* call style the *manner* in which the writer expresses his or her basic attitude toward an event. Today, we label these different manners of expression or styles by terms like "Theater of the Absurd" when referring to an Ionesco play or "Theater of the Ridiculous" when referring to a Charles Ludlam play. The characters, the sets, the costumes, all the aspects of the production aid the playwright in making their attitudes known.

It is particularly important for the actor preparing for an audition to pay attention to style. If I am going to audition for one of Shakespeare's comedies, I will be sure that I have done a complete vocal warmup; the language demands it, and I'd realize I couldn't give a successful audition if I did not warm up. If I'm auditioning for a Neil Simon play, I better be able to understand the structure of a joke and know how to build and deliver one. However, because Simon's work is naturalistic, its vocal demands don't require the same intense attention. Molière's work requires attention be paid to language, movement, and timing.

Knowing the style of the piece for which you are auditioning helps you to prepare appropriately and to make the script work—which is what "they" want. For example, if you are auditioning for a role in a realistic drama, and you speed up the tempo and play a caricature instead of a character, you are in trouble. The style of a text suggests what the tempo should be, the physical dimensions of the people and their surroundings, the demands of the language, and the nature of the characters.

Because actors' careers hinge on their ability to audition well, such knowledge is gold. So you can imagine my glee when, after I had analyzed hundreds of pieces of commercial copy, I discovered a pattern not only in the writing but in the acting directions offered by the auditioners. I began to be able to predict what kinds of direction I would get in the studio by looking very carefully at the script. There was a logic to the chaos after all.

I found that copywriters chose specific writing styles in order to sell their products in specific ways. Once I could identify the different styles, I could come up with some very good answers to the question, "How do I make this material work?" and consequently to the question "What do they want?" What they want is a performance style that matches the writing style. It is just like the theater. You aren't going to get cast in a play by Tennessee Williams if you are approaching the material as if it were a Noël Coward comedy.

I began to formulate a classification system for these manners of writing. I call them commercial styles. I gave each style a name to help my students remember what each one requires in performance. There are three major styles:

- The film style

- The sitcom style

- The "Honeymooners" style

Although each style occurs in every form—some more often in certain forms than in others—I will use a slice-of-life scene as the form with which to illustrate how these styles operate. I'll include sample commercial copy for each style and tell you how to recognize it. Most importantly, I will outline the acting style that each writing style requires.

FILM-STYLE COMMERCIALS

The following commercial script is a classic example of the film style of writing (as with many commercials in this book, I've changed the product name).

The Film-Style Scene

Dan: So, little brother. Did you have a good
    year?

Brother: I'm surprised Dan. The business really
    took off.

Dan: Surprised? I'm not surprised. When everyone
    else on the block had a regular lemonade
    stand, you had lemonade on wheels. And you
    even did your own advertising. That was
    pretty inventive.

Brother: I was only eight years old.

Dan: Oh, come on. Remember you needed the money
    to buy a bike, you started a newspaper
    delivery service. Ollie, Willy, and Sam
    delivered for you, and you called it. . . .

Brother: All bark and no bite!

Dan: And then you all worked an extra year
    because you didn't want just any bike. You
    had to have the best bike. You were never
    willing to settle for second best. . . . By
    the way, did you ever get that computer you
    were talking about?

Brother: It was a tough decision! But after
    looking around I went with the company I
    felt offered me the most support.

Dan: Let me guess! You went with TBQ.

Brother: Right. How did you know I'd choose TBQ?

Dan: For the same reason you bought the best
    bike.

Question: How do you recognize commercials written in the film style?
Answer: The characters' story implies ideas about the product, not facts.

Notice that Dan and his brother's story does not offer much information about the computer company but focuses on the character of the person who chooses it. We don't find out hard facts about the product—whether it's cheaper, better serviced, available in designer colors, or on sale. We don't get a demonstration of its capabilities. Instead, the script implies that the sort of person who chooses TBQ never settles for second best and is innovative and hard-working. Film-style stories are about the characters, their experiences, and—if presented in a scene—their relationship, not about the product. The product's benefits are implied, and the commercial's central idea—innovative, hard-working people who want the best choose TBQ—is communicated through a story that pushes viewers' emotional buttons instead of engaging their logic. The feelings engendered by the story are more important than the facts: Don't you want to be perceived as innovative? Don't you want to be admired and congratulated? Don't you want the best? If so, TBQ is for you.

The writer wants the audience to recognize the characters, identify with the experience, and vicariously participate in their story. Let's analyze the script. It shows us two brothers and tells us that Dan is the older. The only clue about their ages are the words "little brother." Remember, no word is wasted in a commercial script. If the word is there, it is there for a reason; copywriters haven't got the time to overwrite. More importantly, in all forms, most of the acting clues are to be found in the adjectives and adverbs. The fact that those words "little brother" are used affects every creative and marketing idea in this script. Those words identify the relationship and define the market.

As we've learned, the commercial script depends upon stereotypical relationships for quick viewer identification. Older brothers and younger brothers—what is the stereotype? Like the earlier class survey on "librarian," my class surveys on this relationship are almost unanimous: Usually older brothers lord it over younger brothers when they are small. The little one can never do anything right. As they grow older, a rapprochement happens. The older brother begins to accept his younger sibling and relate to him as a peer. Perhaps this scene is just that moment of acceptance.

If I choose that perspective, I have a nice little subtext to play. The little brother (notice he hasn't been given a name) is hearing acknowledgment for the first time, and Dan seems more concerned with letting his younger brother know how he feels about him than finding out which computer he bought. The older–younger idea positions the product for the bright young business person who is on the way up. It's being sold to the young entrepreneur, not to the corporate veteran.

What are the performance requirements of this style of commercial? The film style requires a *naturalistic* film-acting style. That means:

- Physical and vocal expression are sized to the perceived real space between the characters.

- The language is the ordinary diction of everyday life.

- The tempo is appropriate to the circumstances.

- Your script analysis must focus on identifying the character's action. What is the character doing?

- In performance, the character(s) must have an emotional point of view about what they are doing.

For our sample computer commercial, I can almost guarantee that the acting instructions you hear from your auditioners will be something like this:

> They're seated on the patio during a family gathering. They live a distance apart and haven't seen each other for a while. They like each other. Dan is proud of his little brother's achievements. Keep it very conversational. Don't act. Be real.

There is nothing in that direction you shouldn't have known already, except for the detail about where the action is taking place. However, if I take the direction seriously and "don't act," I'll fail in this audition. This style *is* about acting—good solid film acting.

This style is the dominant one among character spokesperson commercials. The same criteria for identification, analysis and performance apply.

THE SITCOM-STYLE COMMERCIAL

We have all watched TV situation comedies, and actors are so familiar with this kind of television entertainment that they hardly think about it as a style at all. All they want is to be starring in one.

The sitcom-style commercial is a marvelously intricate and efficient selling tool that has been around since the very beginning of television, as has the programming it seeks to emulate. I always joke that this style of ad must have been invented by that shrewd marketer, Proctor & Gamble, because it is such a selling machine.

Take this style at its word. It is a *comedy* that arises out of the *situation* the characters find themselves in, not necessarily out of the characters themselves. For example, Frasier, in the NBC series' lead role played by Kelsey Grammer, is a funny character, but the ongoing humor of the series arises out of the situations in which that character finds himself. Basically, he never changes, the circumstances do. Commercial scripts in this style, though not always as amusing as the client might hope, are meant to entertain as well as sell.

Viewers are supposed to feel free to smile or chuckle at the characters' situation—however, we are never meant to laugh *at* the characters themselves.

The world of the sitcom is a fantasy world. You know from the beginning of a *Murphy Brown* episode that, no matter what the situation, everything will turn out all right. Right now, as I am writing this chapter, the show's heroine has discovered that she has a lump in her breast. Even though the writers are dealing with cancer, there is still a laugh every few lines. And I have no fear that Murphy will not recover. She'll be fine. It's a sitcom.

In sitcoms, the sets are bright, the beds are always made, and the characters are comfortably middle-class. The characters never suffer from any of the seven deadly sins; pride, greed, lust, and all the other dark sides of the human personality are merely made light of. The network chief on *Murphy Brown* is laughable in his ambition. Murphy's jealousy is never lastingly destructive to her or anybody else. Everybody is really nice and really likes everybody else. The central characters, male or female, never change, episode to episode. They are usually solving the problems of the other slightly more eccentric or problematic people who surround them. They always relate to these characters with love and humor. They may get "stressed out," but they never get realistically grudging and angry. It's not what these characters think or feel that matters, it's what they do and how they do it that entertains us. There is no subtext in a sitcom. What you see is what you get.

The sitcom commercial in a scene format is always peopled with the same kinds of characters. No matter the sex or name, the two major players are characters that I will call the seller and the buyer. The *seller* knows about the product and its benefits. The seller is a stand-in for the client and represents the client's point of view. That is why that character can never be the object of our laughter. Because the seller is identified with the product, he or she will have very limited acting choices and must remain nice. No matter how outrageous the buyer's behavior, it never offends, it only amuses the seller, who handles the buyer with an attitude of love and humor.

The *buyer* represents the potential consumer. He or she doesn't know about the benefits of the product and, as a result, has an actable problem—a headache, for example. The buyer has his or her problem solved by the seller.

Sellers, relating to buyers in the same way as sitcom heroes relate to those lovably nutty characters surrounding them, solve all problems with a healthy dose of good-humored helpful information. However, one essential ingredient is added—a demonstration.

A Sitcom-Style Scene
Steve: Hurry, Hon! You're late for night school.
Barb: Sure you can handle this whole mess?
Steve: Your new husband is a laundry whiz.
Barb: You'll need a lot to get this clean.
Steve: Just some Nu-Day!

Barb: Some whiz! You'll need powder for whitening, spray for grease, liquid for collars. . . .
Steve: But Nu-Day has ingredients that do all that. Cleans your whole wash all by itself.
Barb: Nu-Day does more than my powder?
Steve: Yep. Cleans more than your liquid, too.
Barb: Even this grease?
Steve: Sure.
Barb: Husbands! Do it my way!
Steve: But. . . .
Barb: Bye.
Steve: Wives! Nu-Day's all I need. . . .

(Quick fade-out, then fade in)

Barb: Great job! Jeans . . . collars . . . really clean! See, you did need all my things.
Steve: All I used was Nu-Day.
Barb: C'mon! What about that grease?
Steve: It's gone.
Barb: Nu-Day cleaned all this?
Steve: All by itself. Guess you found a new detergent.
Barb: Guess you found a new job.

Well, there you have it—another classic. Steve is the seller. Barb is the buyer. Steve has all the information about the product. The demonstration is literal. Before the tablecloth was washed with Nu-Day it had grease on it; after washing, it didn't. This is a simple before and after demonstration—accomplished with the help of the fade-out and fade-in to suggest the passage of time.

Not only is the tablecloth cleaned, but the character of Barb has her actable problem solved as a direct result of the demonstration. When I work on this piece in class, I always ask my students what they think Barb's actable problem might be. Most often, I get answers like these:

• He won't do it her way

• She doesn't believe he can really do the job

• She's late for school and his stubbornness is making her later.

But remember, everyone has to stay likable. After all, Barb will become a Nu-Day user. The sample choices that my students offered would all tend to put the couple into a confrontation over laundry. Barb might appear bossy, whiny, or pushy. Those choices don't keep Barb "nice." You've got to keep the buyer and the seller nice no matter what you do.

The clues to making the more appropriate acting choice are in the description of the relationship and the situation. A newlywed leaving her husband with the laundry to go to night school? First, the stereotype of newlyweds suggests that they haven't learned to argue seriously. They are in love. But the situation has the young bride walking out on her husband—at night—and leaving him with the laundry. How must she feel? A little guilty, of course. Luckily, Barb's guilt is relieved when she sees how well Steve did. In fact, she feels so free of guilt, she gives him the job permanently.

Question: How do you recognize commercials written in the sitcom style? *Answer:* First, there is always a demonstration of the product. Second, if it is a scene, one of the characters is changed by the demonstration, while another character who knows the product guides the demonstration. If it is written in monologue form, the character uses the product and demonstrates its benefits; the monologue speaker is the seller.

What does this tell you about the performance requirements? The sitcom-style commercial demands that:

- If I am playing the seller, my character must always relate to the buyer with warmth, understanding, and light amusement. All my acting choices are positive. If I'm doing a character spokes in this style, I am friendly and have a sense of humor.

- If I am playing the buyer, I must find the actable state of being that results from my lack of knowledge about the product—insecurity, worry, confusion, and physical discomfort are but a few. Notice all these states produce behavior.

- The tempo is that of comedy. Cues are picked up quickly, so there is no dead air between the lines. Remember, the story is about the situation, so the audience watches what the characters do. They don't watch the characters think. The character spokes moves briskly as well.

- The physical values are slightly larger than life, particularly for the buyer. Since the writing centers on the product, I am going to have to show the audience the relationship values—being sure, for example, that as the seller I touch the buyer early in the scene to demonstrate a caring relationship.

- Because it is basically comedic in tempo, the script requires a *button*. A button is an improvised line—or a line coupled with a movement or gesture—that punctuates and ends the performance. The button is the responsibility of the character who does *not* have the last written line. The button is upbeat and positive. Character spokes copy is often "buttoned" with a gesture.

Of course, the language is the speech of everyday life and appropriate in projection to the distance between the players or the audience's perceived distance between the actor and the camera.

I'll take bets on the kind of direction you'll hear at auditions regarding this script:

> They have a great relationship and banter back and forth all the time. They're a hip couple. Be conversational and have fun with it.

This all comes after they've told you the story.

In my opinion, this scene form in the sitcom style is the most difficult of all. There is just a lot to accomplish. Later, when we get into the discussion of scene technique, I'll give you some tricks that will help make them work.

"HONEYMOONERS"-STYLE COMMERCIAL

Laughter is a powerful tool—and weapon. Directed toward ourselves, it makes fun of our frailties and helps us accept them. Directed toward others, laughter denigrates and sometimes wounds. Directed toward our circumstances, it helps keep us sane. Humor is much beloved by the writers of commercials, and through the years they have developed several traditional ways in which they use humor to sell products or define characters. In what I call the "Honeymooners" style, humor—and the laughter it produces—is used and generated in very specific ways.

> *"Honeymooners"-Style Scene*
> Wife: Harry, you've been gone for hours. Didn't
>   they have a muffler for your car?
> Harry: I shoulda gone to A1.
> Wife: Harry, did you get a guarantee this time?
> Harry: I shoulda gone to A1.
> Wife: So how much did you spend? Was it very
>   expensive?
> Harry: I shoulda gone to A1.
> Wife: So tell me, Harry, how come you didn't go
>   to A1?

Poor Harry! He's in hot water. Even so, when we read this script we get the urge to laugh. But the situation by itself is not funny. Played naturalistically, this could be an ugly encounter between husband and wife. Luckily, the rhythm of the repeated line "I shoulda gone to A1" suggests that something else is going on. The clue is where the laughter is directed. We are being set up to laugh at Harry. It's okay to laugh at him because he doesn't represent the product! Harry is the dumb schmuck who didn't go to A1. He is getting what he deserves at the hands of an inferior automotive service—and at the hands of his wife. We *should* laugh at him—that's the point the advertisers are trying to make. Setting up the competition, or the people who use the competition, as objects of derision is perfectly alright. In fact, it is mandatory. It is one major way in which humor is used in commercials.

The viewer is not meant to identify with the characters in this kind of commercial. We're not meant to think for a moment that they live next door. Instead, we know that they are caricatures, like Ralph and Alice Kramden. The comedy is broad, physical, and visual—the humor of slapstick, burlesque, and the commedia dell'arte tradition. Here, jealousy, greed, anger, and pride can be acted out as long as they are comically conceived. It is the humor of the comic stereotype: the nagging wife, the wimpy husband, the sleazy salesman, or the kvetching mother-in-law, to name a few.

Question: How do you recognize commercials written in the "Honeymooners" style?

Answer: The characters don't use the product, and the commercial shows what happens to them because of their poor judgment.

What should this tell you about the performance requirements? The script written in the "Honeymooners" style demands that:

- The people in this style are caricatures, not characters.

- The physical expression is larger than life, consisting of stereotypical vocal and physical behavior that is comical. For example, if Harry's wife is the stereotype of the nagging wife, she can have an ear-piercing voice and an unpleasant dialect. She can repeatedly jab her finger into his chest, and she certainly doesn't have to be pretty.

- The tempo requires the speed of the comedy sketch. Cues are picked up quickly. It builds the way it would in a comedy sketch, to the joke at the end.

- As in the sitcom style, the end of the scene, just prior to the blackout, needs a punctuation point, a visual button executed by the person who does not have the last line.

The directions you would most likely hear at an audition for this commercial aren't hard to guess.

> This can be very broad. Harry's a wimp who is feeling really stupid for not going to A1. His wife only makes him feel worse by getting on his case about it. Have fun.

If you've done your homework, you'll know what to do before you get in the audition room.

RECOGNIZING FORM AND STYLE

Analyzing commercial scripts by pinpointing their form and style gives actors their first chance to control the material. Think of form and style as the longitude and latitude of an acting road map; with this information, you suddenly have guidelines for your performance.

Having something of your own to work with, you won't be totally dependent upon the casting directors, some of whom are great and some of whom are just repeating instructions in the same verbal shorthand they received from the agency or director. It is probably more true than false to say that in all of television and film, the actor who is director-dependent is going to have a hard time. Directors and casting directors in the commercial and advertising field know what results they want, but they are not always skilled at helping actors obtain those results. They know the requirements, but not the process. Actors must be able to function as their own directors and bring their performances into their auditions with them. That is why it is so important for the actor to be able to analyze these advertising scripts and understand the way they work.

In the appendix to this book, I have provided an assortment of commercial scripts. I have labeled the form and style for each and tried to pinpoint the features that will help you define them. The ability to read copy quickly and understand its form and style will be your first tool to acting successfully in commercials.

Will every commercial you encounter neatly fit into one of these categories? The majority will, but not every single one. Advertising is an ever-changing industry, and every rule was made to be broken. If you are unsure about the style of a spot, always err on the side of the naturalistic film approach. For example, if you think a spot is in the film style, you're safe. If you think it is sitcom, but aren't sure, choose film. If you think it is "Honeymooners," but aren't sure, choose sitcom. The objective is to impose a stylistic mark on your performance. It will always move you toward specificity. If the auditioners see intelligence at work, they will work with you if you need to adjust your approach.

9

The MOS

When the mind is in overdrive, the body is headed in the right direction.

MICHAEL CAINE

In Chapter 7, we briefly surveyed the three different commercial forms: the slice-of-life, the character spokesperson, and the MOS ("minus optical track"). In the following pages, we'll examine them in detail. We'll deal with the MOS first, because the techniques that the MOS commercial requires are basic to just about everything else.

As I mentioned earlier, many agents mistakenly think the MOS form is the easiest for actors to do, yet it drives actors crazy. It is, in fact, one of the most difficult kinds of commercials to perform, no matter what style it calls for.

The first obstacle actors will encounter is the procedure that most casting directors follow at MOS auditions. For most commercial auditions, there is a script available that gives actors some idea of what they'll be dealing with and what to expect. They have the comfort of words. At the MOS audition, however, there is seldom any information available to you as you wait outside the audition room. Once in a while, one of the better casting directors will type up the MOS story and post it where the auditioning actors can read it. Unfortunately, however, this practice is not the norm within the industry. Most casting directors wait until you are in the audition studio before they tell you what they want you to do. This process often brings out the worst in an actor, particularly if the actor is a newcomer to auditioning for commercials.

LISTENING

The MOS audition, more than any other, depends upon your ability to listen. Everything you will need to know will come out of the casting director's mouth once you walk in.

Most of the time, all the lessons we actors were taught in our "legitimate" acting classes about listening to our scene partners are pushed out the window when confronted with the pressures of the audition. In the first moments inside the audition room, our minds are usually occupied with inner chatter that goes something like this: "She doesn't like me! Why am I here? Everyone outside is taller, younger, has more hair, [choose one] than I do!" While we're evaluating the competition or trying to read the casting director's thoughts about us, valuable information gets lost.

The first thing we must do is *concentrate* and listen to what the casting director has to say. Block out the static, address the task, and listen! This is the first part of the work. It isn't fancy, but it is essential.

The ability to listen—accurately—is not a common skill. After I lecture my students about the importance of listening carefully, I immediately offer them my imitation of a casting director and recite this typical MOS commercial description for a headache-remedy audition:

```
You're walking down the street.
It's a beautiful day.
You feel terrific.
You discover you don't feel so terrific.
You discover you have a headache.
You discover you have a bad headache.
```

I then ask my students to repeat the story to me. Amazing things happen. First, steps in the story get skipped. Going from feeling terrific to having a bad headache leaves out two vital plot occurrences. Secondly, the describing words get watered down. "Beautiful" becomes "nice," "terrific" becomes "good" or "fine." The only descriptive word that they seem to remember correctly is "bad."

Their responses reveal their tendency to water down the emotional stakes. Even though actors endlessly hear about the necessity for high stakes in their acting classes, they back off and neutralize the very words that have all the acting gasoline.

What do I mean by acting "gasoline"? I mean words that tell me how I feel—terrific, frantic, sleepy, silly, uncomfortable, embarrassed—and/or how I am doing what I'm doing—cautiously, eagerly, enthusiastically, guiltily, skeptically, and so on. These words are adjectives and adverbs, the describing words of the English language.

So now it's time to start talking about language.

LANGUAGE

Although actors don't speak lines in MOS commercials, language plays a pivotal role in the process of performing them. There is a script, but, as I've stated, it is most often orally communicated at the audition by the casting director. Listening for the descriptive language used by the casting director is crucial.

Trained actors are verb-oriented. Their training emphasizes actions as the key concept. The concept of doing and behaving rules their fundamental thinking about their craft. The "-ing" words give them their primary juice. Characters have objectives, and they must *do* things to achieve them. What is the character's immediate need or want? That is his or her objective. What does the character do to get it? That is his or her action. These questions dominate an actor's script analysis.

These are also concepts to be considered by the actor in commercials. But in commercials we must think about them a bit differently, and I'll say more on this when we get to the character spokes copy, in Chapter 11.

Whether for stage or film, adjectives and adverbs found outside the dialogue are ignored in the preparation of a role. We are specifically taught that the writer's descriptions of behavior should be banished. Meisner is quoted as saying:

> If the script says, in so many words, "She begins to blush," cross it out. You cross things like that out because they are anti-intuitive. Those words in parentheses underneath the character's name in the script, like "softly," "angrily," "entreatingly," or "with effort," are aids for the readers of plays, not for actors of them. Cross them out immediately.

This is helpful advice when it comes to longer forms, where you have time to explore what your impulses uncover for you and have an opportunity to test them in the larger arc of the text. But it is exactly the opposite in the commercial. Descriptions are taken literally. The description of how the character is performing the action or feels about performing it and the words that describe any of the nouns—*new* husband, *little* brother, *soft* as silk—have implications for understanding the stereotypical relationship, the tone of the delivery, or the way in which the actions are expected to be performed. We do not have time for intuition. The script, the casting director and the director, all name the result they need to have, and your job is to do it now! And yet, no matter how fast the result must be accomplished, it must look intuitive and spontaneous.

Since commercials are compressed stories that have few, if any, substantial actions to play, your acting clues are not going to be found in the verbs. As in poetry, everything is going to be in the description. I am reminded of *Language in Thought and Action,* a book by S. I. Hayakawa, the great linguistics expert. I remember being surprised that he discussed the language of poetry and the language of advertising in the same chapter. I had never thought about their similarity before (although I had heard people joke that if Shakespeare were alive today, he would be writing ad copy on Madison Avenue). The goal of poetry is to reveal new ways of seeing and experiencing people, places, things, and events. It uses descriptive devices like similes, metaphors, and hyperbole to expand our vision. For example, the Shakespeare sonnet that begins, "Shall I compare thee to a summer's day. . ." goes on through the rest of the thirteen lines to expand upon that initial comparison. Advertising does the same thing. Once the product's identity is established in the copy, the rest of the words tell us it is cheaper, faster, better, delicious, scented, or more beautiful. When actors analyze commercial scripts, they must regard the descriptive words as their major source of appropriate acting ideas.

Since no word is wasted in the commercial script, if the first line is, "I was afraid to go the doctor," you can be sure that the descriptive word, "afraid" is meant to be taken seriously. It's how the writer wanted the character to feel. Not only must you take it seriously, but you must never water it down or reinterpret it as "I was *uncomfortable* about going," or "I was *nervous* about going." Those two ideas are not the same as *afraid*.

Watering down of acting ideas is the same as lowering the stakes—a criticism that has been leveled at many an actor in other acting work. The writer has been very specific. The actor must be as well. The story won't work if that component is missing. And if you can't make the story work, you won't get the job.

There is a good reason for an actor to keep the stakes of the language high: The body and voice will respond to simple but vivid describing words. Those words come with behavior and feelings attached to them. My body instinctively knows how it behaves when it feels terrified or terrific. I just need to think about, imaginatively buy into, that idea and the body will start to express it, just as it did in the "Hickory Dickory Dock" exercise in Chapter 3.

If I focus and engage the mind, the behavior will follow. I don't even need to monitor the reaction. I can trust the body to do the job of making that idea—"afraid to go the doctor"—known. What I must monitor is the strength of ideas that I choose to focus upon. If I focus on low-octane ideas like "nice" or "happy," I will not receive enough gas from those ideas to power the engine of my body. "Thrilled to pieces," "ecstatic," or "terrific" are much more specific and emotionally loaded descriptions and, therefore, more likely to produce behavior. In fact, "nice," "happy," and even "excited," are so overused and lacking in emotional meaning that they are banned in my classroom. As my students have heard me say a million times, "If you put Pablum in, you get Pablum out."

Mad, Glad, Sad: An Exercise

Here's an exercise I usually assign my students. Not only will it be helpful for your work in television commercials, but it will feed your imagination as you work in other performing media as well.

The goal is to create a written list of words or groups of words that describe feelings. One way to do it is to start by organizing descriptions of the shades of feeling of "mad," "glad," and "sad." Write these three emotional states across the top of a blank piece of paper and then list every synonym or phrase that is a nuance of that description in a column underneath. For example:

MAD	GLAD	SAD
belligerent	ecstatic	morose
enraged	exuberant	inconsolable
disgruntled	enchanted	surly
incensed	overjoyed	gloomy

This is one way to investigate the many wonderful nuances of feeling that humans experience. (By the way, shades of these three emotions always appear in audition scenes for soap operas.) Another way to do the exercise is to make an alphabetical list of all the descriptions that you can come up with. For example, the letter "D" has many—defeated, degraded, dejected, delighted, and so on.

You needn't do this all in one sitting. It should be a process that continues as you stretch your acting imagination. Sanford Meisner told his students that their emotional instrument is like a piano with eighty-eight keys, with each key serving as an emotional note. It is your job to investigate those notes and learn how to play them. One way to test whether you have a good describing word is to test it in the sentence "I am _____" or a sentence that has the past or future tense of the verb "to be." If it successfully completes the sentence, then you know you have a good word choice. For example:

"I am enchanted."
"I was inconsolable."
"I will be enraged."

Another test is to try your list of words in the "Macy's Information Booth" exercise described in Chapter 5. If the describing word you choose produces behavior in that exercise, then you have an actable idea for a commercial text.

I hope that you now understand the danger in taming descriptive language. If, as an actor, you have this tendency to neutralize vibrant words and make them more beige, I'll bet you don't indulge this habit only when working on commercial scripts. It's just easier to spot this habit when the text is short. I guarantee that if it is happening in the analysis and execution of commercial text, it is happening in other texts as well.

It seems to me that this watering-down impulse springs from actors' desires to stay safe. Perhaps they feel that this keeps them from being wrong or from overacting. This is a misguided opinion. It only strangles your imagination.

LISTENING AND MOS DIRECTIONS

Let's return to the sample MOS headache audition from earlier in this chapter. Once you walk into the audition and are listening carefully, what are the key elements of the story that you must hear?

- *The plot:* What happens and in what sequence, in this case, goes something like this: "I'm walking down a street. I start out okay and then get a headache that becomes progressively more intense."

- *The describing words:* In this example, they are "beautiful day," "feeling terrific," "discover," and "bad."

- *The major transition:* This is the most important change in the commercial story. Most MOS commercials—but not all—have one. It is like the climax of a play: Everything leads up to it, and everything is different after it. The contrast provided by the major change highlights the story's message.

Let's look at this last point more closely. The sample MOS story is an illustration of the way in which a headache can ruin a great day, and it employs the film style described in Chapter 8. You need to identify the major transition because it gives you the emotional arc of your performance. The major change in this piece is between "I feel terrific" and "No, I don't feel so terrific." Everything after that is a more intense degree of not feeling terrific. Therefore, "terrific" to "not terrific" is the transition, full of contrast. For you, the actor, this means that the feeling terrific part must be extremely clear and strong in order for the subsequent idea—"No, I don't feel so terrific"—to produce a readable change in your face and eyes.

In most commercial scripts, the major change, if it occurs, happens close to the end of the story. That structure allows the actor to establish an emotional line and build on it till the point of transition. Keep that in mind as you look at the MOS examples provided in the appendix to this book.

THE MOS STORY AS INNER MONOLOGUE

If you really understood the "Hickory Dickory Dock" exercise, you realize that behavior is a result of what is going on inside your head—that thinking is doing that makes believable behavior happen. No one in the Hickory stories had to indicate or purposefully gesture in order to communicate. The physicalization was spontaneous and appropriate to the thought and its emotional content. This is the "real thinking" that Uta Hagen talks about when she discusses how organized thought occurs as the result of "envisaging"—that is, focusing the mind on—a task or a series of mental doings. This is what I mean by thinking as doing.

Focusing your mind on doing something is vital to your MOS technique, and to this end you want to concentrate your thinking on an inner monologue. We know that in everyday life our minds are always evaluating the world around us, as if we were talking to ourselves in a series of questions and statements: "Was that the doorbell?" "No, it wasn't," and so forth. In order to perform the MOS story, to bring it to life, we are going to create an inner monologue made up of *high-stakes* questions and statements. Then we are going to focus on it and talk to ourselves using its words.

It is critical that you trust that by committing fully to this inner monologue you will produce the desired result, an appropriate series of changes in your eyes, face, and body—*behavior* that is identifiable to the audience.

To create your inner monologue, you start with the narrative and turn it into a dialogue with yourself. This must be done in language that is *of the moment*. For instance, you should avoid wording your dialogue in the progressive tense: "I am walking down the street" or "I am feeling terrific!" Such dialogue is not dramatic; it's the way we speak when we are standing outside an event and observing it. The language of our thoughts for this monologue should be in the present tense, simple and explicit. That is the tense of the experience of the moment.

The inner monologue for the headache audition would go something like this:

```
Wow, what a beautiful day!
I feel terrific!
No, I don't feel so terrific.
What's wrong with me?
Damn! I have a headache.
It's right behind my eyes.
And it's a beaut!
```

If you focus on talking your way through the story *internally,* something appropriate will happen *externally* in your eyes, face, and body. The camera will see you thinking, evaluating, and solving. You may not even have to put your hand to your temple in order to indicate headache. If the casting director wants it, go ahead, but try to do the movement as a result of your internal monologue. That way, it will be perceived as organic behavior, not as indication. It will appear to be motivated by the discomfort of the headache, and not seen as an artificial gesture that the actor has added to make sure that the audience gets it.

MOVEMENT AT THE MOS AUDITION

One of the two issues that remain to be discussed is the literal doing of this sample MOS story—walking. If you were auditioning for this commercial and had a question concerning how much action the auditioners wanted, you should ask the casting director. "Am I walking in place?" "Am I permitted to walk into the frame?" Casting directors welcome intelligent questions. They want you to do a good job. They're on your side (surprise, surprise) and will always clarify the actions to the best of their ability. They have set up the audition; they know what they need to show the director.

It seems that today's auditions are getting more complex in terms of movement and activities. This is very tough on the actor who has to juggle all the elements on such short notice. In a soft-drink MOS audition that was held recently at my studio, the casting director was auditioning for an actor to portray a rock band manager at a concert. In the final shot, he was to be moving through the backstage corridors, acknowledging performers as he quickly made his way. To approximate this, the casting director set up a door unit (a movable prop door) for the entrance, and a series of turns and moves to help create the feeling of backstage hustle-bustle. The trap was that most of the actors had to concentrate so hard on doing the choreography of the audition that their acting went out the window. It seems to me that some advertising agencies have little knowledge of what an actor can accomplish in a commercial audition and, consequently, expect casting directors to produce unrealistic results in the time they have to spend with the actors in the studio.

In some MOS auditions, the casting director will "talk you through it." This means that he or she, after telling you the whole story at the beginning, will cue your actions *as* you perform the actions. You must listen carefully for the information you need to create your inner monologue, particularly the clues for the emotional arc. When the director cues you, you'll be told things like: "Go to the window," "Turn toward the camera," "Sit down," or "Cross." These directions are helpful with the plot, but the motivations or intentions that enliven the story are up to you.

PROPS AT THE MOS AUDITION

The other important element of the MOS audition—or any audition—is the prop. When I have my students work on this headache ad in class, they generally begin the action without any thought of the given circumstances. I am always forced to ask them if they walk down the street carrying nothing. Invariably, the answer is "no"; they carry briefcases, backpacks, or pocketbooks. So I always tell them to get the item and use it.

So equip yourself with props whenever it is appropriate to the circumstances. Stella Adler said, "The prop will keep you truthful." It keeps you truthful because it anchors you in space and forces you to handle the object with natural behavior. Even if you are miming a walk for this audition, the bookbag over your shoulder will make you walk a specific way. Don't forget that most audition studios or spaces are excruciatingly empty. Anything that helps ground you in that void is an asset, particularly when it assists you in creating believable behavior. Just be careful in the commercial audition to invent with what is at hand.

Also remember that in order for the prop to be accepted by the casting director, it must be appropriate to the circumstances and enhance the meaning of the action. If it doesn't, you won't be allowed to use it, for it can become distracting rather than illuminating.

TASTING: THE DELICIOUS MOS

Numerous commercials feature actors eating and drinking. Think about the ingestibles that are advertised: fast foods, snacks, soft drinks, breakfast foods, frozen and convenience foods, cake mixes, coffee, tea, desserts, and food staples like butter and flour. In most of these scripts, tasting the food or drink— the hero product or Brand X—will be essential to the story. (Alcohol, although advertised, will never be consumed on-camera; it's against the law.)

The clients take the tasting moment seriously. One well-known coffee advertiser took it seriously enough to make a videotape consisting of out-takes from the company's completed commercials, demonstrating both good and bad sniffs and sips of their product. They distributed the tape to casting directors as a guideline for their expectations in the audition.

The conditions of an actual commercial shoot are not the same ones you'll encounter at an audition. When it comes to tasting, the realities are very different. It is far easier to taste the product and create an appropriate response at a shoot than it is at an audition. At the shoot, you really have the product to put in your mouth, although no one expects you to eat or drink the product during take after take after take. The producers will provide you with what is affectionately known as a spit bucket. The camera shoots you putting the burger into your mouth and having the reaction that the director wants. If you watch commercials carefully, you'll generally see a cutaway soon after that moment—the camera cuts away to another image. That cutaway allows the actors to spit whatever product is left in their mouth into a bucket so that they don't have to swallow it.

Shooting the product or the reaction to the product is the most time-consuming part of the day on the set. No matter how much you might genuinely enjoy the food or beverage you are ingesting, your stomach couldn't take the strain of having to eat it in large quantities.

Even though you may never have to swallow on the set, at least you have the real product to feel and taste in your mouth. This is not the case at the audition. Auditions involving food and drink are notorious, perhaps because the client is cheap and does not want to foot the bill for a hamburger for every auditioning actor, or because the casting director is too swamped to invent suitable substitutes. My general experience at these auditions is that nothing to eat or drink is provided for the actors—except the occasional dry, stale soda cracker pieces they use as a substitute for that supposedly luscious entree.

I once had such an audition at a major New York advertising agency. The script opened with the mother—the part I was auditioning for—tasting a freshly baked cookie made by her daughter and being unimpressed. The script had me ask my daughter if she had used butter in the recipe. I told her that butter would make them better, and then we moved on to a shot of us at a party enjoying the cookies made with our hero—butter. As you can see, this script called for two tastings, one negative and one positive. At the first audition, there was no real cookie to put into my mouth and taste. At the callback, there still was nothing provided to taste but air. I am sure that this agency and their very capable casting director had a good reason for this, but such circumstances do not aid the actor. Instead, this kind of setup invites poor miming even from good actors.

How do you deal with the reality of an audition like the one I just described? If they want to see believable behavior no matter what the circumstances, then you give it to them. You create believable tasting behavior, shaped any way they want it, because you know that acting is behaving.

Tasting Behavior
"*Tasting behavior*—what's that?" I assume you are asking. In my classes where I have a video setup, I answer the question with the following demonstration, which uses a little bag of M&Ms and several small bags of flavored potato chips. I ask an actor to go to the mark in front of the camera. I give him an M&M and tell him not to look at it. I then ask the actor to put it in his mouth and tell me the color of the coating by tasting it. The camera records what

happens. Then I ask another actor to go to the mark, and I give her some potato chips. I ask her to taste them and rate their saltiness on a scale of one to ten, ten being the highest. Again the camera records what happens. I may have another actor taste for spice, another for greasiness. After I've recorded all these tastings, I have a demo tape of tasting behavior.

Amazingly, all the actors do the same thing. Viewers will say that they see the actors thinking, or they may have noticed that the demonstrating actor's eyes were "looking around." Each actor displayed similar behavior. As they put the food into their mouths—sometimes as they approached their mouths with the food—their eyes would move from their outward and forward focus to either the upper left, upper right, or to the lower corner of their eye sockets. Once the actors had evaluated the M&M or potato chip and answered the question I'd asked, their eyes would leave that private place and once again focus outwardly toward the questioner. It was as if their eyes went inward to look at the food in their mouths, as if the taste buds needed the eyes in order to have the sensory experience.

This kind of visual behavior happens whenever the mind is receiving sensory input. Our sight is the most highly developed of our five senses. Our eyes go to wherever the stimulus is being received, whether it be through touch, taste, smell, or hearing. We believe behavior when it reminds us of what we have seen under similar circumstances. We are so accustomed to seeing people display this kind of visual behavior in connection with a sensory discovery that if it doesn't happen we disbelieve that they had the experience.

Knowing and understanding the way your instrument works is going to help you produce a believable tasting experience, even though there may be nothing in your mouth. Let's look at the four steps in this behavioral process: the approach, the taste, the internal or MOS response, and the outward communication.

1. *The Approach*. In tasting something for a commercial audition, you have to pick up the product and convey it to your mouth. Your behavioral approach is determined by how you feel about tasting the food or beverage in question. Are you skeptical? Are you eager? Are you in the midst of a routine? Are you quietly expecting a good experience? Perhaps your internal monologue might consist of: "I'm not sure . . . ." "Can't wait!" or "Coffee! What a lovely idea."

2. *The Taste*. This is the moment when you put the food or beverage in your mouth and your eyes follow it there. Think about it in exactly that way. Imagine that your eyes follow the food from your lips to your tongue and to the roof of your mouth.

3. *The MOS Response*. What is the response the director wants? Is it positive, negative, pleasantly surprised, unpleasantly surprised, or satisfied? These are just a few of the possible choices. While your eyes are focused inside,

use the internal monologue again. It can be simple, consisting of one word or just a sound: "Wow!" "Ahh," "Mmmm," or "Yuck!" Remember what I said earlier about contrast? If I had to do a ""Yuck!" response, I would probably choose an inner monologue for my approach like "Can't wait!" or "Coffee! What a lovely idea!"

4. *The Outward Communication.* This depends entirely upon the circumstances you've been given and the style of the script. The communication may range from a realistic private moment acknowledging the source of your pleasure or disappointment to a spoken response to your scene partner. The response could be a combination of both nonverbal and verbal outward communication.

One important point to remember is that you must always swallow. Although you are given no food or beverage to work with in the audition, these simple physical steps followed by a swallow produces the believable behavior that fools the viewer into thinking that you tasted and ingested the product.

You don't have to wait to speak until your mouth is empty. That's what your mother told you to do, but it does not help you to create believable behavior or maintain the necessary tempo.

The manner in which you handle the food is another way to make the illusion more potent. Pay close attention the next time you eat a huge hamburger with all the trimmings. How do you hold it? Observe the problems that kind of food poses. Other foods may be piping hot, may drip, or may get all over your face. Study the ways in which you handle and eat different types of food and drink. Be ready to integrate this behavior into the audition.

The style of the script should help shape your internal monologue choices

| *The Approach* | *The Taste* | *MOS Response* | *Outward Communication* |

Tasting Behavior. *Tasting is a behavioral process commonly acted in commercials. You want to be able to perform these four stages and be natural—and don't forget to swallow.*

so that your performance is appropriately physicalized. Take a commercial in which you are asked to taste a cup of coffee. If the spot was written in a film style, the outward communication might be as simple as "Mmmm"; if it was sitcom style it might be "Mmmm, great!"; and if it was in the "Honeymooners" style, it could be as big as "Fantastic!"

Today, a large number of MOS commercials are conceived in the film style. The audition is directed that way. However, don't expect the final televised version to resemble what you were asked to do initially. Unfortunately, some clients get nervous on the set and decide that "more" is needed. What began in a naturalistic film style now gets bumped up to sitcom size. These last-minute cold feet lead to final productions that are not quite what the creative team had in mind. However, on the set give them what they want. Once you have the job, don't question why—simply deliver the performance.

Perfecting the discipline of the well-executed MOS is rewarding. It provides training in specificity and concentration, if nothing else. It demands that you be in the moment from the moment that you walk in the door. Most importantly, it is the first step in understanding what words can do for you and what they cannot.

10

The One-Liner

Words are preceded by an immediate source
and sent with an immediate need.

UTA HAGEN

It may seem a little strange to devote a chapter to commercials that consist of one line of dialogue, a line that is sometimes only one word long. However, while the auditions for these short, simple commercials can be quite frustrating, a large percentage of commercials are based on just this type of script. Better that I warn you ahead of time and give you some tips on coping with them.

THE THREE-IN-A-ROW AUDITION

Actors auditioning for one-line commercials are likely to confront the peculiar practice of having to deliver them "three in a row," a custom that often proves intimidating to the uninitiated. In such a situation, casting directors want each auditioning actor to slate his or her name and then deliver the one line three times consecutively with the aim of making each reading different and distinct. The camera will not be turned off between the three readings.

Your auditioners in these instances may or may not specify whether they would like the readings to be different; but if you want to make an impression at your audition, you had better make them so. If you don't, you'll sound like a parrot repeating the same words over and over again as if there were no thought behind them. Also, they'll want your readings to appear natural and spontaneous. Of course, you must deliver the goods without much time to prepare.

In order to pull off this performing feat with consistency, actors should be friendly with a few basic camera and acting concepts. As elementary as they may seem, they are the skills that are frequently jettisoned in the adrenaline-rush of auditioning. Simplicity demands courage.

As with the MOS, one-liners demand that you strip your acting technique to its bare essentials. Remember how the MOS required you to focus your thinking through the inner monologue? That technique guides you toward using words as a means to achieving an end, instead of using words as an end unto themselves.

The one-liner's successful execution results from the actor's ability to trust the mind-body-voice connection: As Michael Caine says, "If you trust your character's thought process, your face will behave normally." **You must understand how the actor's instrument behaves.** You saw in the MOS chapter that once we understood the visible behavior that accompanies the sensory experience of tasting, it became a powerful tool in creating the tasting illusion.

The one-liner also offers actors the opportunity to practice fast preparation. Therefore, it demands that actors be able to quickly choose a "moment before"—that is, the moment that is previous to the line, in which something happened that causes a reaction in the present. We'll examine this idea just a little later.

Most of all, the one-liner audition demands risk. You have got to make a choice and go with it. No evaluating, no changing your mind, no hesitation— just *go!*

As in the MOS, the best way to eat this elephant is one bite at a time. So let's take this audition apart and look at its individual components. Once the challenges are understood, then you have a chance to conquer them.

CHOREOGRAPHY

First, let's deal with what I call the choreography of the audition. By *choreography* I mean a sequence of physical movements—like blocking on a stage— that helps the auditioning actor separate each of the three line readings from one another so they can be perceived as different. I agree with Michael Caine on the following point: Get the physical moves memorized first, whether on the set or at the audition. Let the body get the feel of the movements before you add the lines.

When you are not making eye contact with the camera, it perceives you as existing in a private world. You use this fact to separate each of the three readings so that they appear as completely different moments. Here's the routine:

1. Slate into the lens—a nice and friendly, glad-to-meet-you introduction. ("Hi! My name is Joan See.")

2. Take your eyes away from the camera lens, as if you were going off the stage.

3. Bring your eyes back into the camera when you say the line. ("Thank you, Smith-Jones.")

4. Take your eyes away again.

5. Bring them back into the lens when you repeat the line ("Thank you, Smith-Jones.")

6. Repeat steps 4 and 5.

The choreography will also help establish the appearance of *spontaneity*. So will your effective use of your voice and gestures.

THROWING THE BALL

To the physical separation of each reading you are ready to add the voice and gestures that will make each moment appear spontaneous. For your audience to believe you as a real person having a real experience, they must see your behavior as responsive.

As a rule, behavior is a *response,* or reaction, to a prior stimulus, and that stimulus is received through one of the five senses. If that stimulus, that pinch, requires a conscious response, there is a momentary thoughtful evaluation of it. During that momentary evaluation the eyes focus inward, even if only for a millisecond. In order to voice the mind's findings, the body releases a breath. It moves up and out, toward the object of the communication. The eyes respond and follow the breath outward. This movement of the eyes attached to the release of the breath creates the look of spontaneity. So now let's add that to our basic choreography.

1. Slate into the lens as before.

2. Take your eyes away from the lens and into your privacy. (This is still the same as step 2 above.)

3. This time, in privacy, release the breath and start to speak. The moment the "th" sound of "Thank you, Smith-Jones" starts, move the visual focus from your privacy to the outward focus, the camera lens. Don't delay the release of your breath until your eyes make contact with the lens; release it just before eye contact. This way, your eyes are in motion as you start to speak. Attach a mid-body gesture to the breath release to get the feel of its movement away from you. You get the spoken response started in privacy and then give it away to the camera.

4. Finish the line into the camera. Don't stop and take another breath as you connect with the lens. It should feel a little like you are tossing the communication away from you.

This little "dance routine" allows the viewer to see you *as if* you were entering the television frame in action. You'll appear to be responding to some stimulus from the moment before you spoke. You are not standing eyeball to eyeball with the camera reciting lines with different inflections.

A Throwing-the-Ball Exercise

For anyone having difficulty understanding this technique, try the following exercise. Get a soccer ball or basketball and stand opposite a partner. Use a nursery rhyme as your text. As you voice the first sound of the first word in the first line, throw the ball to your partner. Try to imagine that you are attaching that sound to the breath and the motion of throwing. Feel as if the rest of the sounds/words are attached to the ball as it moves away from you. The ball must leave your hands as the first word leaves your lips. Have your partner return the ball, and go on to the second line. This exercise should give you the feeling and rhythm of having a thought, putting it on the breath, and then releasing it out into the world.

THE MOMENT BEFORE

Once you are comfortable with the external, physical blocking, it is time to move on to the internal, emotional work. How do you get those line readings to be different? How do you get them to be natural and spontaneous? The immediate answer is that you don't get that result by focusing on the words. You get that result by focusing on how you, as the character, feel in response to some *stimulus*. The stimulus is a trigger for an emotional response, not a verbal response. For example, I see a man sitting in a car outside my house. Am I surprised? Frightened? Delighted? Puzzled? Words may follow, but the emotion, or feeling-response, is first.

The auditioning actor needs to conceive of a feeling-response that will come from the given circumstances of the script. That is, you must imagine the moment in which your character, in privacy, experienced a stimulus before the one-line spoken response.

In real-life moments, a stimulus creates a feeling-response that may or may not lead to the spoken response. We respond to something we *hear, taste, smell,* or *see.* So the crucial question is not what the stimulus we experience makes us say, but how it makes us feel in the *moment before* the line. We decide how the character needs to feel based on the realities of the circumstances given in the script. However, here's where we run into one of the fundamental differences between acting in the theater (and theater-based acting classes) and acting in film: preparation time.

The Impulse

As a young actor, the concept of the *impulse* was one I didn't understand. Like many others, I thought of it as some mysterious occurrence that was prompted by a visiting muse. Not until I had the good fortune to study with Sanford Meisner did I begin to get an idea of what an impulse might be. Working and watching others in his class, the fog began to lift a little. This great teacher found all sorts of creative ways to make us, his students, use our heads in order to leave them behind.

Meisner got us to focus on the "emotional river" upon which the text floated. He then helped us to have the courage to undam the river and release it. In that release, the river was pure and free from the controlling mind. I watched and experienced feelings triggered, released, and made known to the world through the body and the voice. How marvelous. How simple. The body and the voice were always ready to reveal me to the world.

The voice is one of the marvels of human anatomy. The fact that breath passes over and through some specialized tissue and is capable of creating so many sounds is amazing. More amazing is the way it makes sound that expresses our feelings. Just sigh or laugh and you'll understand what I mean.

When we are responding to the world around us, we are responding with the body and the voice. Both are always in motion before the word is shaped. It is the vocal behavior, including tone, pitch, support, projection, and texture, that cues the listener to what is going on emotionally in the speaker.

Recognizing that feelings have sound, that you can express a feeling through a sound, is vital to our next step. Ask yourself what sound you might make if you were asked to make a frightened sound, a delighted sound, a puzzled sound. Remember in Chapter 9, on MOS commercials, when you made lists of words that describe feelings—the adverbs and adjectives that are the "gasoline" fueling a performance? Just by thinking those high-octane words, you can get ideas about a sound as well as a physical life to accompany it.

Keeping that in mind, let's go back to our sample one-line audition. In this audition, the casting director has told you the following:

> You're a successful young businessperson who has been investing regularly with Smith-Jones. Their good work for you has resulted in your ability to purchase a wonderful home. This line, "Thank you, Smith-Jones," is what you want to say to them. Give me three in a row.

Your first question to yourself is how would you feel under those circumstances? You are the character, after all. It is *as if* you were getting your $20,000 down-payment check today. The question should not be: "How am I going to read the line?" or, "How can I look like a successful businessperson?" The question is simply, *"How would I feel?"*

Here's where your "glad" list of gasoline words should be very helpful. You might feel "thrilled to pieces," "relieved," or "surprised" to be getting a $20,000 check today. Now ask yourself what "thrilled to pieces" would sound like. To put it another way, ask yourself: "What sound would I make if I were thrilled to pieces?" To discover the sound, do not only think "thrilled to pieces," but imagine being "thrilled to pieces"—buy into the feeling. Say it out loud several times: "I'm thrilled to pieces, I'm thrilled to pieces, I'm thrilled to pieces." The body and the voice will come quickly to the aid of the mind. They will rush to express the idea in sound and physical behavior. The feelings you've attached to the words will be known through the sound of your voice and the look on your face. As in the "Hickory Dickory Dock" exercises you've done before, the impulse appears so fast you're hardly aware of it. You can trust that it will; you don't have to do anything.

So the way to get the feeling into the line is to get the *sound* of the feeling. Having the thought is not enough; it has got to be made into behavior if it is to communicate. Here the behavior is vocal. The release of the breath/sound is the vocal instrument's response to your need to communicate. It takes what is happening on the inside and makes it known to the outside world. On that breath/sound release your feeling moves away from you toward the target of your communication.

Now let's go back over the steps for a three-in-a-row.

1. Slate into the lens with a friendly introduction.

2. Take your eyes away from the lens and into your privacy. Get the sound of the feeling you wish to communicate. As soon as you hear the sound start, drop the words on the breath—that is, release them. Don't control the way they will sound. Let go of them.

3. As you make the first sound of the first word, bring your eyes into the lens, as if you are giving the line to a person. Finish the line.

4. Go back into your privacy.

5. Repeat Steps 2 and 3. Do everything the same way with the exception of the "gasoline": Choose an alternative high-octane acting word to use for the second and third readings. Make sure you get the sound before you begin.

It is vital to the success of this approach that several things happen. First, you must drop the words on the breath. The impulse will shape the reading. It does in real life. Why shouldn't it now?

Secondly, you must not take another breath between the initial impulse and saying the words. If you do, that second breath changes the feeling you communicate, as if you were expressing a different impulse.

Thirdly, you must not hold back. As in the ball exercise, once you start to throw, you are committed; there's no changing your mind in midstream and taking it back. Once you choose the feeling and the sound is started, you "throw the ball." If you hesitate, you'll fracture the illusion of spontaneity.

This audition is all about doing your homework and then giving up control of the result. The result will be what it will be. The way the words come out of your mouth will be spontaneous and believable. Driven by your need to respond, they communicate your feeling-response, rather than some need to stay safe and in control.

ON THE SET

This way of working with one-liners is invaluable once you've wowed them at the audition and are working on the set. Remember that film scripts—whether for commercials, television, or features—are shot in pieces. Many times, you are shooting a single line of dialogue. Unfortunately, it is an opportunity for everyone on the set to have an opinion about how the line should be said.

I once did forty-seven takes of one line. We did it every possible way and then some. Relying on thought-and-sound concept of the impulse saved my life. Because we were shooting so tightly, I couldn't use the rest of my body to help. If I had tried to do preplanned readings, I would have gone dead by the tenth take.

There is also a lesson here for the larger script. Every scripted role starts with one line, even Lady Macbeth's. An old friend tells a story that illustrates this point. She was theatrically trained, and when Hollywood called, she was working on Broadway. She had not done any camera work up until that time. The film was a Western, and she was the lead ingenue. The first scheduled shoot was a highly emotional scene that required her to be almost in tears at the top. She arrived in the morning, went to hair and makeup, and then sat quietly and began her emotional preparation. However, as often happens, there was a technical problem and the scene was delayed. She went off into a corner and began to prepare once more. The scene was delayed again. After a break for lunch, she started her preparation once more. Then the generator blew. When they were finally set to shoot her scene in the late afternoon, she tried to get emotionally ready once more but found that her preparation had all dried up and nothing would happen.

The moral of this story is that all acting in film requires that you be ready and prepared to deliver a performance when the film crew is ready to shoot, not when you are ready. If you can't make it happen when they need it to happen, it's your problem. Lengthy and baroque preparations do not serve you on the set. They certainly don't serve the audition, particularly the commercial audition.

The good news is that you don't need all that time. Once you connect the body and voice to the mind and really trust that they're ready to communicate for you on a moment's notice, you can really fly.

My friend had attempted to prepare the whole emotional line of the heroine's character where instead she might have used her body and voice to execute the emotional point of view of the opening moment of that one particular scene. In those mini-scripts we call commercials, the attention paid to the moment before and the impulse it creates is one of the linchpins of success. In that moment, your acting gasoline is ignited and your motor turns over.

Here we have an opportunity to experience the difference between the intellectual process of preparation and the organic release that creates a seemingly uncontrolled result. In reality, you control your performance by your ability to conjure up and be in a "moment before" and your ability to release the feeling-response it creates. (Take a look at some of the sample one-liners in the Appendix.)

Practicing the technique needed for this audition provides you with an opportunity to learn how to pack your parachute, jump, and freefall in all kinds of acting jobs.

11

The Character Spokesperson

To be is to do.
PLATO

Now we turn to the commercial form that actors dread: the spokesperson, or *spokes,* for short. These are the spots that consist of wall-to-wall copy. At the audition the copy is often badly hand-printed on shiny cue cards and that make us feel like Bambi in the headlights. There are so many words. Where do we begin? We forget that every journey begins with a single step, and every piece of spokes copy with a single line.

To refresh your memory: You can always recognize the spokes form by the fact that a single character talks either to the camera or with the camera, and you can tell by the script's use of pronouns which kind of spokes is which. "You" and "yours" predominate in the former; "I," "me," and "my" in the latter. These I-me-my scripts, meant to be delivered as if they were conversations, are the ones we will focus on in this chapter; those written to be delivered to the camera will be discussed in Chapter 13.

REAL CHARACTERS

These scripts in which the actor talks with the camera are meant to be perceived as little personal stories told by real people whose feelings are essential to the ultimate success of the sell. Remember, characters are perceived as real only if they are perceived to have feelings.

These days, these ads are likely to be film-style. As we've discussed, advertisers have discovered that "real people" with "real feelings" sell better than stiff announcers obviously paid by the company offering the product. Remember the research mentioned earlier: Our feelings about a product or service represent a large part of what builds brand loyalty. We remember how we feel about things more than we remember the facts about it.

The character spokesperson says all the words while the camera functions as the second person in what could imaginatively be called a scene—it becomes your acting partner. This is exactly what happens in the shooting of a film when your scene partner returns to the dressing room while the scene is shot from his or her point of view. You are left to play the scene with the camera, *as if* your actor partner were still there.

This fact about the way one-camera technique works has led many a teacher of commercial technique—in search of a conversational delivery—to direct the actor to "see somebody in the lens." This direction is supposed to help the actor imagine a substitute partner to whom his or her delivery of the copy seems just as real and conversational.

Early on in my career in commercials, I tried to work with the copy this way, and when I started teaching I tried to encourage my students to use this approach as well. Unfortunately, my experience with the "substitute" was discouraging. Sometimes you can hold on to the substitution, sometimes you can't. But the substitution was not always enough to create an energized and believable performance. You can personalize the camera any way you wish and cast it as anyone you choose, but that idea alone is not enough. I can know who I'm talking to, but the thing that matters is *why*.

"See someone in the lens" is a direction that burdens the actor. Well brought up actors really try to do that. However, the only time I've seen someone in the lens is when the camera was in so tight for a closeup that I could see my own reflection. Let's face it, the camera, the lights, all the technical stuff which are always in your field of vision, will always look like technical stuff.

The solution is to treat the camera as if *it* were a person, and not struggle to imagine a face in the lens. This is the key to turning the camera into a friendly scene partner, as opposed to an adversary that must be changed. Even if you can't achieve a workable *as if,* you can always decide why you are talking to the camera itself. It is always *as if* the camera were gifted with the ability to respond. The continual presence of the camera is what makes this idea so important.

THE FORM

Ninety-nine percent of the time, character spokes commercials are directed to be friendly, one-to-one, intimate, and real, with a thrown away quality—a little like an interview, but always conversational. To achieve this desired result, we need to further explore the form.

In other books about commercials that I have read, the copy has been broken into sections that have been given nice but technical advertising names. For example, one book breaks the scripts down into categories like attention-getter, problem, solution, reason, resolution, and close. In general, this analysis provides a decent description of the writing, but it isn't very useful to most of the actors I know. The actor in an androgynous spokes role (see Chapter 13) or the voice-over announcer can more easily use these ideas than the character spokes actor.

If you break the copy into neat sections like "attention-getter," the words become an entity unto themselves. They exist for the purpose of the advertiser's objective—selling the product or service. In that case, the words are not the result of an experience that happened to *you,* the speaker. And as we've noted, actors cannot be perceived as real if their words don't seem to emerge from their past and move them forward into the future. They cannot be perceived as real if what they are doing doesn't have some emotional color to it.

Therefore, it's imperative that you treat this kind of spokesperson material as if it were a piece of theatrical writing. They are mini-monologues and are best analyzed as such. Because the actor in character spokes is supposed to be "talking to a friend across the kitchen table," the form could also be defined as what Uta Hagen calls a *duologue*. The camera, sitting in as your imaginary acting partner, possesses the capacity to respond to your words *as if* it were your friend. You have all the words, and your scene partner, the camera, cannot change what you want to say. The story is about you.

Treating these scripts as monologues, we are going to look at them as having not technical sections but acting sections called *beats*.

BEATS AND OBJECTIVES

For the definition of the term "beat," I subscribe to what the fine actress and teacher Alice Spivak calls them: small objectives within a scene that serve the major objective. An objective, of course, is what the character wants or needs. We are back to why the character is doing and saying what he or she is doing and saying. The answer is to satisfy that want or need. That is the character's reason for being in the scene.

My major objective in a scene may be that I want to find out the truth. I may never say so directly to other people in the scene, but that is why my character is there. Within the scene I will have different ways of going about achieving my goal. I may want to *confront* someone; I may want to quietly *confide* in someone; I may want to *cajole* someone. Each section of the dialogue in which I want to *do* something is a beat. My wanting or needing triggers actions taken in order to achieve my goal. Each of these beats and their actions support my major objective of wanting to find the truth.

Actions are what a character does. They produce behavior and stimulate feelings. An action is always expressed in the form of a *verb* : I *confront,* I *confide,* I *cajole.* I like to add *-ing* to the verb to describe what the character is doing in the scene: confronting, confiding, cajoling. For me and my students this makes it easier to understand and, therefore, to accomplish. Expressing the idea in this verb form puts the action in the here and now. It describes what I am doing right now. It is not what I have done or will do.

This action idea is the focus of most of an actor's theatrical training but generally it's never applied to commercial texts. Yet in spokesperson copy, it's a magical idea. Think about it. Nothing really happens in a commercial. People talk to other people "across the kitchen table," or they talk to the camera. Movement is fairly static, and the biggest activity might be eating a hamburger. The actor stands there with "nothing to do" except read the cue card. The only action involved in that is reading, and the only feeling stimulated by it is discomfort.

The idea that the beats—those small sections of the copy—can be made active by deciding what are you doing with the words within each beat can transform your performance. In the beat, do you:

• Justify your behavior?

• Admit a mistake?

• Confide a secret?

• Brag about your smart move?

These are what I call verbal actions, and once you start to address the task of really doing them, a lot of problems get solved. You will be present and in the moment, and your energy level will be appropriate for the action you have chosen—never too much and never too little. You won't even have to think about it.

When you see the result of playing a verbal action you'll see why it's not enough merely to know to whom you're talking. That information cannot guarantee focus and energy. You need to know that the words in the script are meant to have an impact upon your off-screen partner. They will only have an impact if the words are communicated for a reason, if you focus your energy on doing something with them.

Knowing you are focused on what you are doing with the words, you'll be energized and alive. The power that the committed doing of a task has on your performance will save you every time. So always know what you're doing more than whom you're talking to. The first approach produces results ninety-nine percent of the time, the other is truly hit or miss. And don't worry about the imaginary face in the lens.

Once you know what objective you are acting upon in each beat, you'll strengthen the golden thread between you and the lens. The more you focus your attention outside yourself and on what you are doing in relation to the camera your acting partner, the more the viewer will pay attention. Think of the camera as your partner, imagine that it loves this kind of attention. That's how you make it feel like it's really a person.

STRUCTURE

The character spokes commercial has a time-tested structure of functions of specific beats. When you understand how the script is put together and how the pieces function you'll have a better handle on what you must do.

The script is divided into at least three sections: an opening beat, a middle beat, and a closing beat. There may be more than one beat in the middle section, but there will always be at least one. Their purposes will be made clearer by considering the expository essays we were taught to write in high school and continued to churn out in college. The ideas in the essay were organized into paragraphs. The opening paragraph delineated the topic to be discussed. The middle paragraphs, called the body, gave us more information about the topic: examples, experiences, and descriptions, for example. Then the closing paragraph summed up all the information and drew the conclusion about the topic.

The beats of the character spokes script function the same way as the paragraphs of the essay. The opening beat is the topic—the subject of the conversation. The middle beat, or beats, give you more information about the subject. Each will have its own reason to be there. It may "justify" your position, it may "describe" what you did, or it may "defend" your choice. The last beat sums it all up by making a point about the subject.

If you use this three-part template for dividing the copy into actable pieces, you'll be more able to define what you are doing in each beat. You'll become aware that the script is not just one big wall of words. It will become far more manageable and less intimidating.

THE GLUING IDEA

Realistically, every commercial's super-objective is to have impact upon the viewer in a way that sells products or services. But the actor can never play the super-objective. It is not actable. The actor in on-camera commercials must always start from a position of not selling, just telling.

Successful theater scripts have an idea or thematic message that ties all the beats together. In a play the theme is an expression of the writer's view of the human condition made manifest through the characterizations and actions of the play. In a commercial script, it may be difficult to discover what view of the human condition is being expressed. For our purposes the point made in the closing beat can be enough to hold the 28-second story together. Searching for larger and more universal themes can often present the actor with an analysis struggle that has little payoff.

The most useful question I have found to help me discover more about the writer's intentions is: *Why* these words in the mouth of this character for this product? This tends to get me to the "gluing idea" really quickly. Later in this chapter, we'll discuss the importance of asking *Why* questions in analyzing copy.

THE MOMENT BEFORE THE BEATS

All doings are, as Uta Hagen says, "responses to time, place, the environs, and/or interaction with your partners." Nowhere is that information more important than in the first beat of any dramatic piece. I wish I could tattoo the phrase "moment before" on the inside of every actor's palm like a test crib-sheet. It is, almost without fail, the first thing actors leave outside the room— that is, assuming they know what a "moment before" is. To my chagrin, I frequently hear actors who are working on a character spokes script explain the moment before by describing their character's socioeconomic status or what happened to the character yesterday. All of that is part of the homework, but none of it is actable. Yes, you have to know who you are and where you are, but it is the stimulus—heard, saw, smelled, tasted, or touched—that you receive in the moment before you speak that makes you speak. That stimulus causes you to consciously evaluate it and triggers feelings about it. I react to the stimulus because I need to, and my response to the stimulus is my first action.

For example, after reading a particular character spokes script, I decide to imagine that in the "moment before" I'm to say my first line, my imaginary scene partner has accused me of lying. Consequently, I feel attacked and act to defend myself. Since the camera is my stand-in partner, it is *as if* the camera has accused me. I respond directly to my scene partner, the camera, by defending myself.

What is the pinch that happens in the moment before that causes the ouch of reaction? If you can imagine the pinch, you'll discover the ouch by asking yourself how the pinch makes you feel and what it makes you want to do. Lots of times the clues to your imagined pinch can be spotted at the very beginning of the commercial. For example, the opening line, "You ask me how I feel about being a working parent?" makes the stimulus in the moment before obvious—the character heard a provocative question that she wanted to answer. That was a *heard* pinch.

The opening line, "A policeman never forgets the first highway fatality he sees," suggests that, in the moment before, this character witnessed another highway fatality—that was a *seen* pinch.

The more attention actors give to choosing a strong moment before, the better they will be propelled into the first beat of the mini-monologue, and the more momentum they will have to carry them through the rest of the spot.

My definition of the moment before differs from the definition that is espoused by Michael Shurtleff and acting teachers who specialize in longer texts. Their description of this moment means creating, as you do your homework on a character, a fully realized and specific emotional state which propels you into the action. Your specific feelings are in response to your history and your needs at that point in the text.

Because of the very nature of the commercial script—it's compression, one-dimensional characters, and representational stories—Shurtleff's moment before can take too long to prepare; besides, the actor doesn't have very much history from which to create it. And the actor in commercials is obligated to serve the specific emotional tone asked for by the casting director and/or mandated by the text.

But like the teachers of longer texts, I *am* talking about entering the dramatic action in a specific emotional state. And for that state to appear rooted in a former experience it has to be a feeling-response triggered by something. Uta Hagen in her discussion about actions says, "What is done to you by someone or something causes your reponses, your sensations and your feelings, about which you will want to do the next thing." Remember, your moment before is what is done to you by someone or something—those stimuli

—that cause you to respond with action. These stimuli happen in the exact moment before you begin your action and infuse your action with an emotional point of view. You must structure that "pinch" so that it triggers the specific feeling-response required by the commercial. This will anchor your performance in real behavior.

NEXT: THE OPENING BEAT

The opening or beginning beat of the commercial duologue tells us the subject of the conversation—what we're going to talk about. It also parallels the description that Alice Spivak gives of the opening beat of a scene: "The first beat is brief, and it springs you into the scene out of the previous circumstances."

The opening beat of the character spokes commercial is exactly that: It is brief—one to two lines at most—and it springs you into the duologue out of the previous experience.

The technique we learned for one-liners now helps in the longer monologue. Remember the release—the making of a sound and releasing it with words attached to it? The same kind of release, and the ensuing feeling of being propelled into and through a line, is the springboard into the entire script.

As you will recall, you prepare for the release in the moment before, and that response to the stimulus brings you into the frame with purpose and presence—in action; you'll already be committed to doing something. This should capture your listener's attention and carry it into the main sections of the story.

The opening beat establishes the subject of the conversation. Remember, you have not started the conversation to sell a product, but to tell a story. Here are some typical opening lines, each serving as the initial beat:

• You ask me how I feel about being a working parent?

• Ever notice how fast things change when they change?

• All my life I've been pretending to know something about wine.

• A policeman never forgets the first highway fatality he sees.

• My son, home from college not one day and already with the questions.

There are no attention-getting headlines in these opening lines, just the beginning of a conversation. The topics about to be discussed are:

• The feelings of a working parent

• Change

• Lying

• Highway fatalities

• A son and his questions

Notice there is not a product or service name to be seen. Ensuing beats will expand upon the topic and, in the course of the conversation, the character spokesperson in each of these scripts (the full scripts are in the Appendix) will tell us about:

- A great child-care service

- A soap for older dry skin

- A popular domestic wine

- Safety belts

- A breakfast cereal

This premise is crucial: *The product is part of the story, not the reason for the story*. Thus, your acting choices should be based on the characters, their story, and their circumstances. The story is a device for amplifying and demonstrating ideas and facts about the product. We can act the story. We can't act the product.

The first beat and its trigger—the moment before—should demand your greatest attention in preparing for an audition. If these two things are crafted well, you will most likely "get" the rest of it. If you don't know what your character is responding to and why, nothing else matters. Allowing the breath to push you through the first line and avoiding cutting that line up into little pieces in order to be dramatic is essential.

MIDDLE BEATS

The beats in the middle of the script describe events, explain reasons, and justify actions. They give us more information about and understanding of the conversation's subject by describing and explaining the specifics. They answer the questions posed by the opening beat: what were the feelings of the working parent; what changed for the character and how she feels about it; what the character lied about and why; why the policeman never forgets; and what were the son's questions and how the father handled them.

Interior beats give the characters an opportunity to express how they feel about the topic and tell us what made them feel that way.

ENDING BEATS

In most cases, the ending or final beat will tell us the reason why the person told us the story—the point. For example, the commercial that begins "My son, home from college not one day and already with the questions," ends with "Phi Beta Kappa and he can still learn a thing or two from his old man." The character told us the story in order to make the point that father still knows best—at least about breakfast cereal.

One of the common errors made in this material is for the actor to weaken, or "wimp out," in the last beat. Energy goes and the voice turns soft and/or gets unconnected to the breath. The pace is picked up and the line is thrown away. There is nothing conversational about this. I almost always feel as if the actor sensed the end was near and wanted to hurry up and finish so he or she could leave the studio. This is not a way to make a point unless it is about your nerves.

MORE ON VERBAL ACTIONS

Again, consider the importance of the verbal action: Every one of the beats in your mini-monologue has a reason to exist and that reason is to *do* something. What you are doing with the words in the script is the question. The answer "talking" is never good enough. There are many kinds of talking and you do them all the time. "Talking" is not a specific description of a communication. "Gossiping" is specific; "apologizing" is also.

Really engaging and doing the verbal action connects mind and body and puts you in the moment. You cannot think about yourself if you are focused on an action. The verbal action moves you forward from moment to moment in a logical progression. Doing something triggers behavior and behavior triggers feelings.

Here are a few examples of verbal actions that are useful in commercials:

confiding	complaining	confessing
bragging	defending yourself	gossiping
describing	explaining	challenging
inviting	apologizing	sharing good news
asking	coaxing	letting the cat out of the bag

As you figure out what your story is about, you will discover what kind of talking is necessary. You won't flounder in character spokes material if you've chosen strong verbal actions with which to tell the story. I mean verbal actions that bring feelings with them, that involve emotions. For example, "confessing" implies that you are feeling guilty; "sharing the good news" implies that you have experienced something amazing, thrilling, or delightful; "apologizing" often occurs in response to having made a mistake. I have found that "sharing" is a very usable verbal action. Sharing a secret, sharing your unhappiness, sharing any one of your feelings works extremely well.

On the other hand, I recommend you avoid "convincing" and "teaching"— they will distance you emotionally from your audience. When all else fails, "admit." This is a wonderful choice from Mira Rostova's list of twelve moment-to-moment doings. It seems to intensify the viewers' sense of the actor's vulnerability and humanity.

I have used it in my own auditions and had it produce extremely good results.

CHARACTER

It cannot be said too often that in film, on television, and especially in commercials, you are what you look like. For example, if you have an audition for a "young mom," the only character work you need to do concerns superficials—wardrobe, hairstyle, makeup. That you are at the audition in the first place means that the agent and the casting director agree that visually you are believable as a young mom. So don't try to act like a young mom—that is not the assignment. Very, very seldom, if ever, will you be asked to play anything against your physical type in a commercial audition.

Certainly, embracing the stereotype of the young mom by wearing the appropriate wardrobe, hairstyle, and makeup is going to help make your "look" more specific. But your major acting attention is going to be focused on the gasoline words suggested by the script, the casting director, and perhaps the agent. How do they describe the young mom? Is she bubbly, frazzled, laid back, confident, worried? When your agent uses descriptions of your character like "upscale," "blue-collar," or "casual," he or she is referring to styling, not to an acting choice.

Ninety-eight percent of everything you need to know will be found in the copy. However, the elements of the story that we still need to read and listen for are the given circumstances: *when* and *where*.

WHEN

When the action is occurring is a big consideration in most theatrical material. Not only the literal time of day is of importance but the historical period in which the action takes place has a great impact upon the nature of expressed relationships, motives, and social psychology. However, most commercial scripts deal with contemporary society, so the historical period rarely poses much concern.

The question of when in character spokes commercials involves a consideration of when the event being talked about happened. In a great number of mini-monologues characters talk to the camera about experiences that happened to them in the past. A character tells us about something that happened before he or she started to speak, rather than speaking to us as the event is occurring.

Where you are in a time-relation to the event you are discussing is very important. If you're telling us about how you got a headache yesterday while babysitting for your sister's kids, and how it disappeared when you took the hero aspirin, then you do not have the headache at the moment; you have no pain in the moment of telling the story. Actors who get fixated on acting choices based on product believe a line like "My headache was killing me!" demands a demonstration of intense pain. They completely overlook the fact that the line is written in the past tense. The line is a simple statement of what happened yesterday. It is a remembered headache—I don't have it now—and that should stop me from demonstrating the severe pain of yesterday.

The Retelling Script

In all scripts that *retell* an experience, you must be aware that you are describing past events and, more importantly, describing feelings that occurred at an earlier time. Trying to dramatize and recreate those feelings is not only impossible but bad acting. The truth is that we never experience an event, and its attendant feelings, with the same intensity that it had when it happened. As we get some distance from an event and the feelings that surrounded it, our perspective changes. Time and distance blur the sharp edges of unpleasant or painful circumstances and tend to suffuse pleasant ones with a heightened golden glow. Experiencing past events with the same intensity they had in the moment would "blow our circuits" and drive us mad. Perspective protects us.

In these commercial mini-monologues, nine times out of ten the chronological distance from the event allows the character to have a sense of humor about it. The humor is self-deprecating, growing out of the character's recognition of what a silly goose he or she has been in the past. This is one of the classic ways in which humor is used in the creation of commercials, and I call it the "Silly Goosedom" device. If you refer to the Appendix 3, you can read three commercials that are retellings and employ this device: "Beauty Soap," "Wine," and "Ketchup." In these, a character recalls past behavior: getting upset about what her mother thought; faking a knowledge of wine; and running around like a crazy person. All situations are talked about through the prism of past time and the realization of present wisdom. These are characters with whom the audience is meant to bond.

This kind of gentle, self-directed humor gives characters human frailties and consequently allows the viewer to better identify with them. The characters were not wrong to be upset, to fake it, or to run around like a crazy person—just silly geese who have become enlightened. Casting directors often give you a clue about what to do when they direct you using the phrase "you (the character) have a sense of humor about it."

In a retelling script, the closing beat will often tell you the emotional state that resulted from the experience the character has just described. That is the feeling state you may need to bring in at the beginning. The feelings that were engendered as a result of the events in the story may indeed be what the character wishes to share.

The cereal commercial in Appendix 3 is a good example of how the closing beat gives the actor a clue to the character's feelings at the opening. The father is pleased with himself over how he handled and won the past confrontation with his son—"Phi Beta Kappa and he still can learn a thing from his old man." Therefore, his feeling in the opening line—"My son's home from college not one day and already with the questions"—does not suggest annoyance. The father knows when he recounts what happened that he won. He is really pleased with himself, and his eventual victory tells us he's still top dog.

WHERE

The consideration of place is another important given circumstance that actors must use to make character spokes copy more believable. If the where is important to the story, it will be alluded to in the copy or implied through the dialogue and action. Imaginatively conjuring up the specifics of the setting is your job.

Approach the work the same way as you would if working on a scene (see Chapter 12). Know where everything is and, if the story needs it, make us aware of the product by referring to it visually and physically.

Creating an environment for yourself is important. Many casting directors have begun to recognize the need for at least a minimal set and a few important props in auditions. I am sure their clients appreciate the more specific look of their audition tapes. I hope they also know how helpful it is to the actor.

The audition space is foreign and scary at best. Anything that can anchor the performer in a more positive relationship with that space helps quell the feeling of performing in a void. My only fear about increasingly detailed audition sets is that the people who view the tape will be seduced into expecting a perfectly executed performance—complete with intricate movement and graceful prop manipulation—in two takes.

Some spokes copy does not specify a place. If there is none mentioned, listen carefully to what the casting directors say at the beginning of an audition; they may include a description of where the action takes place in their remarks. Whatever given circumstances are communicated to you by the casting directors, you must try to incorporate them into your performance. They wouldn't mention it if it weren't important. Whether you are in the rain, a large crowd, or a restaurant, the circumstances should affect your behavior.

If no place is specified either in the script or by the casting director, don't invent one. Your auditors won't know what your visual or physical references pertain to. Frankly, it will confuse them. Focus on your verbal actions and the limbo environment will take care of itself.

ACTIVITIES

The rules applying to activities are discussed more in depth in the next chapter; suffice it to say here that activities are minimal in the character spokes form. Inventing an activity just so that you will have something to do at the top of a spot is precarious, because many times you may choose an activity that says nothing about the character or is not appropriate to the situation. It pulls the focus away from what is important. Your auditors then get more involved in trying to figure out what you are doing instead of becoming involved in how well you are communicating their message.

If there is an activity, it most likely will have to do with the product: eating, smelling, or feeling the product and, more often than not, showing us the product. This can lead an actor into the "product trap": Actors who are making choices based on what they are selling might feel obligated to pretend to use the product throughout the performance. For instance, the actor playing the father in the cereal commercial mentioned earlier might feel compelled to mime eating the stuff all through the audition simply because he is seated at the breakfast table with a cereal bowl. As a result, the actor's focus would go from a verbal action to a product demonstration. It will destroy his believability. The product trap will kill you every time. All that may be required is a casual gesture to the box or the bowl.

Another trap for actors occurs when they have to bring the product's package into the frame. An actor's tendency is to bring it into the frame and hold it in place like a display mannequin. Every viewer's eye gets drawn to the package and everyone starts wondering how long the actor is going to hold it there. A word to the wise: Keep the audition focus on you. Don't worry, once you have the job, the focus of the shoot will be the product. In the audition, handle the product casually, get it in and out of the picture with ease, grace, and speed. Believe me, when they shoot the job, they will bolt your arm into place if it is necessary for the product to be displayed to its utmost advantage.

WHY

In the analysis of every script, there is no more important question to ask than *Why*. Your answers to that question put you in the shoes of the writer and the mind of the character. "Why are these words in the mouth of this character for this product?" is a good question to ask as you begin to figure out any piece of copy. It reminds you that the script wasn't written on the spur of the moment. It was crafted logically, following careful guidelines and under microscopic scrutiny.

By asking Why, you may also arrive at your gluing idea. For example, consider that question in relation to our highway patrolman's story (see the complete text in the Appendix). We have to ask: Why a highway patrolman? Yes, highway patrolmen do see those fatalities, but perhaps it also has something to do with the pain that he has experienced in watching a child die needlessly. Seeing a strong man tormented by a parent's stupidity and the ensuing death of the child might give us the gluing idea: Not using seat belts invites tragedy, or "better safe than sorry."

Another question would be: "Why is he telling us this haunting memory"? His entire story is constructed to scare us into using seat belts on ourselves and our children. If the actor does not get the audience to share in the patrolman's pain and frustration, he won't be fulfilling the needs of the script.

There is nothing more logical than a commercial script; everything in it exists for a reason. These scripts are the thinking actor's crossword puzzle. As a thinking actor, get into the habit of asking Why and putting your energy into finding or inventing answers and reasons. This investigation can only help to make your work richer and more grounded. At the very least you will have a better sense of what you are talking about.

Practicing this habit in your commercial work will help solidify it in your other work. Stella Adler said that your talent is in your justifications. There is more than a grain of truth in that idea, particularly in character spokes copy.

"Why do you need to tell me your story?" Remember, if you don't have a reason to communicate, I don't have a reason to listen.

The reasons come out of analysis. Questioning why the copy is written a certain way and why the character is saying certain words helps you be the director first and the actor second. All too often, our actor's twitch gets us focused on knowing the lines before we think of why those lines are there. We set about memorizing the words as if they were the only thing that deserved our attention. But directors need to know why the words happen before they can understand what they really mean. In doing your homework, if you function as director first and actor second, you will be able to change the words into meaningful communication and make the copy work.

12

The Slice-of-Life Scene

Scene: a unit of dramatic action in which a single point or effect is made.

The Random House Dictionary

Of the three forms of commercial scripts described in Chapter 7, the one that actors feel most comfortable auditioning for is in the slice-of-life format. The reasons are simple: The dialogue structure and the presence of another actor make the commercial script feel similar to those they have worked with in acting classes or performed on a stage.

Amazingly, I find that actors abandon the training they say they've acquired in all those scene classes the minute they are confronted with an audition for a slice-of-life commercial. Of course, any audition situation could cause actors to forsake their acting technique, but the unsettling speed of the commercial audition seems to encourage them to ditch the foundations of their craft with greater regularity.

What are the basic elements in scenes? What have you learned about scenes in your other acting classes that may pertain to what happens in commercial scenes? Once you answer these questions, you'll be better able to understand the acting requirements. Here are six elements of slice-of-life scenes:

1. Scripts call for two or more characters.

2. The characters are involved in a communication of factual and psychological information.

3. The characters have a life before the beginning of the scene and a life after the scene has ended.

4. The characters have actions and obstacles to their actions.

5. Characters in a scene have a relationship.

6. Characters in a scene engage in activities.

Now let's look at each of these elements and see how they apply in slice-of-life commercials.

NUMBER OF CHARACTERS

Unlike scenes in a play, slice-of-life scenes rarely call for more than two scripted characters. This is a function of cost. Scripted words make an actor a *principal,* and that entitles the actor to a higher session fee and residuals. There may be more people in the finished commercial, but they are likely to be extras who are paid by the day and hour and are not entitled to rerun fees.

In commercials, the second person or the third person in the scene may be the camera, its lines delivered via an off-camera voice. Here is an example:

> *Off-Camera Second Character*
> ATM Talking Machine: Why are you just using me for my money?
> Man: Huh?
> Machine: Don't you ever pay bills or make deposits?
> Man: Sure . . . at the bank.
> Machine: You're at the bank. I'm your HomeTown Banking Machine.
> Man: I feel strange giving my money to a machine.
> Machine: You don't feel strange taking it.
> Man: Well. . . .
> Machine: Look. I take deposits. Payments. Transfer money. I can give you a receipt. What more could you want?
> Man: How about a song?
> Machine: Sure. (With singers:) HomeTown gives you more.

In this spot, the camera is the bank machine. The dialogue is between the actor and the lens. The actor relates to the camera *as if* it were the bank machine by looking directly into its lens. At the audition, the machine's dialogue will be delivered by the casting director from behind the camera. At the shoot, the lines may be delivered by the actor who has been hired to record the machine's voice. This is the ideal (and we hope the client will pay for it), but otherwise, the script supervisor will read the machine's lines.

Sometimes, the camera will act as a *third* character in a slice-of-life scene. The following ad is a good example.

> *Three-Character Slice-of-Life Scene*
> Voice-over: Kitty and Sandy work together, but they rarely agree.
> Sandy: We agree this is a great place for seafood.
> VO: Because of Sea Feast's amazing smorgasbord?
> Kitty: Yes. Their Supreme Fish Fillets are the best.

Sandy: No. It's their fried clams.
Kitty: What about the fish sticks?
Sandy: What about the Supreme Kabobs?
VO: Ladies, ladies, you call that agreeing?
Kitty: Sure. We agree the smorgasbord at Sea
     Feast has lots of different kinds of seafood
     to choose from.
Sandy: And believe me, that's a big help to
     working people like us.
VO: Stop in at Sea Feast and try the
     smorgasbord. You'll agree it's a great place
     for seafood.
Sandy: That goes here.
Kitty: No, it doesn't.

Here the third character is the interviewer, played by the camera. Dialogue is shared between the ladies, as well as between the ladies and the camera. In both circumstances, the actor treats the camera *as if* it were a real person.

COMMUNICATING INFORMATION

Look at the slice-of-life scene between the recently married couple, Steve and Barb, that I included in Chapter 8 (see page 70). In contains both factual and psychological information. The factual information in that spot is: They're newlyweds. She goes to night school; he has to do the laundry. He knows the facts about the detergent; she doesn't. She learns the facts and changes her position. These facts are found in the script.

The psychological information is: Barb feels guilty about leaving him with the laundry, but Steve doesn't mind. She is relieved of her guilt by the success of his endeavors. The psychological information is communicated through the behavior.

You need to understand the factual information first, because the facts are the clues to the psychological information. You can deduce that Barb feels guilty about leaving Steve with the laundry because of the fact that they are newlyweds. You must do a lot of deducing in commercials because the facts are necessarily few in a script so compressed.

CHARACTERS' LIVES BEFORE AND AFTER

Madison Avenue named the slice-of-life scene exactly: It's a few moments extracted from the continuum that forms the characters' lives. As we've learned, when every scene begins, the characters in it are coming from, and are in the process of responding to, the previous circumstances—the moment before.

If that first moment on-camera is not focused, responsive, and specific, I guarantee that the following 28 seconds will fail. Once again, because of the brevity of the text, you cannot delay character revelation; there's no time for playing catch-up. Everything must spring directly and logically out of what you bring to the scene.

Actors all too often forget that if they leave the scene, they are leaving for a reason; they seemingly believe that once the job of saying the lines is over, they're finished. Nothing more is required, so having said their last line, they drop their energy. Some even look away from the world of their scene to see if the casting director is pleased. It is rather like saying, "I'm done! How did you like me?"

In the Steve and Barb scene, Barb enters from another room on her way to night school. She enters in a specific emotional state based on the script's circumstances—she's late. At the end of the first section of the script, she exits the scene. Again, she leaves in a specific emotional state based on the circumstances—she's even more late.

ACTIONS AND OBSTACLES

As I stated earlier, commercial scenes very rarely call for physical actions. In most slice-of-life scenes, the characters don't do much more than talk to each other. In the Steve and Barb detergent commercial, Barb is trying to leave for night school and Steve's laundering is the obstacle that stops her progress out the door. They then confront each other over the way to do the laundry and, after time passes and a demonstration is made, there is a resolution.

In commercial scripts, the actor is better off dealing with the concept of *events* rather than the concept of actions and obstacles. Michael Shurtleff, in *Audition,* describes an event as a change, a confrontation, or a climax of a scene. He also says that events can be psychological—two characters involved in a power struggle, for example. These happenings change the characters; they make the story progress. Shurtleff suggests that if you can't identify the event, invent one. This may be necessary in a great many commercial scenes. In our sample slices of life, what is happening between the characters is most important. Identifying and playing the subtle changes that happen turns basically passive talk into interesting dramatic action.

The actor in the commercial scene must look for what is happening. The slice-of-life scene featuring an older and younger brother in Chapter 8 doesn't have a written change, confrontation, or climax. We can deduce what the event is from the facts we are given. The older brother *acknowledges* his younger brother's achievements. He is making a friend of his brother. This is a psychological event. (Notice that the product, a computer, plays no part in the event or major action.)

It's the job of the actor to make the script as action-filled as possible. Actors who don't are the often ones that get asked for "more energy" at auditions.

THE CHARACTERS' RELATIONSHIP

The explicitly stated relationship of characters in a script does not contain enough acting information. Mother–son, husband–wife, friends, neighbors—

those are relationship labels, and they don't come with much acting gasoline. It is the description of the relationship that conveys the specific ideas that actors can use—ideas triggered by phrases such as *new* husband, *little* brother, *protective* mother, or *nosy* friend. Remember, too, that in the commercial script we always embrace the stereotypical ideas surrounding the stated relationship.

One of the factors that makes playing relationships so difficult in auditions is that ninety percent of the time your scene partner is a stranger. The Russian roulette nature of the audition situation often precludes the casting director's planned pairings. Actors come late, cancel, arrive early. You get whoever is there when you are.

In the 28-second script, most of what the audience perceives about the emotional relationship results from behavior that they see. Therefore, appropriate physical contact is an essential part of creating the perception of a warm, loving relationship. In our real-life behavior, we not only don't go around touching strangers, we often actively seek to avoid making contact. Therefore, it is really unnatural to expect that we will comfortably touch acting partners we don't even know. And yet you must. That social boundary is best crossed by committing to the doing. You don't have the grace of a rehearsal period to get past your shyness. Physical contact appropriate to the relationship is essential to communicating that a relationship is warm and caring.

What is appropriate? The contact should come out of the character's feeling in the moment of the action, and it should be suitable to the relationship. If we have one newlywed leaving the other for night school, for example, it would be appropriate for the departing character to give the other a quick kiss good-bye on the cheek. Patting a friend on the arm if you are concerned, touching your child's face as you comfort them, all of these gestures would be appropriate. Keep the contact simple. Don't let the physical contact draw attention away from the story.

THE CHARACTERS' ACTIVITIES

Ah, activities! The simple act of really doing something is very powerful. It grounds the actor, and the audience sees real behavior. Finding an activity that is appropriate to the longer theater scene can sometimes be tricky. It is twice the challenge when working in the 28-second slice-of-life scene.

For example, the actor auditioning for the character of the new husband in the Steve and Barb detergent commercial would face this kind of challenge. He is in the frame when the scene starts and has the opening line. What appropriate activity can he do to make himself more believable? The choice of activity should be suitable to and spring from the given circumstances. To do something inappropriate is worse than doing nothing at all.

With luck, the casting director has some towels for the actors auditioning for Steve. If not, the actor can use his own scarf or sweater, or otherwise invented laundry. Any of these would be appropriate substitutes for the dirty laundry at the top of the scene that Steve would be shaking out and inspecting. It would save him from clichéd behavior—looking at his watch to indicate that Barb was late, for instance—and it would undoubtedly seem believable.

But what the actor must do with his laundry prop is *really* shake it out and inspect it. Casually or idly handling the prop does nothing for anyone, let alone the actor who is trying to get the job. Be simple and specific about your activity and personalize each prop. You can do this preplanning outside the room; it is part of your homework. Decide whether Steve is looking for stains, checking out pockets, or just counting the buttons on the sweater—and fully commit to doing them. More importantly, know where Steve drops his activity to focus on Barb. The opening activity is most often dropped when your character is challenged by a scene partner and a new beat begins. In this case, Steve should drop the activity when he responds to his wife's challenge: "Some pro! You'll need a lot to get this clean."

An activity can be dangerous in commercial auditions when the actor uses it as a life preserver—hanging on to it throughout the script. The audition then becomes about the prop or activity and not about the events. My theory is that some casting directors avoid giving props to actors or assigning them activities because so many actors handle them poorly.

When no props are provided in the audition, invent—but keep it simple and *real*. Use your appointment book as a newspaper, for example, and really read it. Really tie your tie, really put on the earring, really buckle your belt, or brush your hair. If an activity is called for, find a simple one that comes out of the situation and character, and then really do it. And always know why the character is engaged in the activity.

THE FIVE Ws

In every piece of dramatic material, even in improvisations, actors use information to prepare their performance. In the theater, we often call the process of finding that information "doing our homework." Out of our homework we weave the history, circumstances, and the motivations of our characters. Our homework is done through the process of answering five questions:

1. *Who* are you?

2. *What* are you doing?

3. *When* are you doing it?

4. *Where* are doing it?

5. *Why* are you doing it?

If you are not acquainted with the five Ws, now is as good a time as any to get introduced. We examined three of them, When, Where, and Why, in the preceding chapter on the character spokesperson commercial. Here we want to consider all five in the slice-of-life scene, for they are just as crucial in commercial scripts as in theatrical scripts. They are your road map to a performance that fulfills the needs of the story.

Who Are You?

When you are dealing with a full-length play, the answer to who your character is can be very complex and multilayered. In the commercial script the answer is pretty straightforward; your character may be a mom, a customer-service worker, a taxi driver. Just as you sought the important part of the answer in the word or words that describe a relationship, you want to find information as to what characterizes you as an individual. Are you a *worried* mom, an *in-control* customer service worker, a *good-natured, talkative* taxi driver? You get these clues directly from the script or from the casting director.

What Are You Doing?

What you are doing in a commercial scene is always best stated by asking yourself what kind of event is taking place. Let's look at the commercial for the Automated Teller Machine earlier (see page 110). This event is a confrontation. We might phrase it this way: "In search of love, a neglected and unappreciated banking machine *confronts* an unsuspecting customer." Notice how high I put the ATM's stakes. The machine confronts the customer, and the customer must then defend his or her actions. Identifying the event—*confrontation*—can lead you to what you are doing with the words, to your verbal action—*confronting*. In commercials, it rarely leads us to a physical action.

When Are You Doing It?

As we've seen, in a theatrical or film text, When not only asks what time of day, but what historical period. The time could be the Jazz Age, for example. In the slice-of-life commercial, When the event is taking place usually will have few implications. Most commercial scenes are taking place in contemporary times.

Where Are You?

As an actor working in commercials you should ask yourself not where you are, but whether there is an environment at all. If there is, what do you need to do about it? In scenes, there will always be specified surroundings. How does that specific environment affect your behavior? The answer can give you lots of information about body language, projection, and the way to handle props.

Some commercial scripts have very explicit environments. Others, mostly mini-monologues, don't. It's easy to surmise that Barb and Steve are in their kitchen or laundry room. However, Dan and his little brother (see page 67) have no scripted environment, and there are no clues as to where the event is happening. What do you do in such a situation? Ask the casting director or assistant. They will have this information if the script doesn't.

Let's say you now know where you are, but at the audition you don't have any set to help put you into a space. You need to decide where everything is in relation to you, even though it is not present. You need to create the set in your mind's eye and relate to its elements *as if* they were present. That means you should physically refer to elements in the environment with a gesture or a look if the script gives you that opportunity.

Why Are You Doing It?

Finally, you ask the most critical question that can be asked by an actor. Knowing why your character does what he or she does—enters, leaves, chooses to do the laundry—will propel you from event to event.

Always give yourself a reason to do what you do. You can imaginatively create reasons using the text as the source material for these discoveries. Your reasons can turn a flatly written scene into an interesting exchange between people.

Outside the script, the casting director will be your only source of information about the five Ws. If the casting director makes a point of giving you specific circumstances, then you must integrate them into your performance. No word is wasted. Every description is a clue to help you understand what you need to do to in order to make the script work.

All the points above are the acting considerations for slices-of-life, no matter what the style of writing. Paying careful attention to answering the five Ws will give you specific objectives for your performance. You will not feel as if you are winging it, and you will begin to take control of the material as you focus more closely on what you are doing, instead of on what you are saying.

THE SITCOM SCENE

Now let's consider at greater length commercial scenes written in the style of the television situation comedy. The sitcom is itself a hybrid entertainment form. Developed for the half-hour time requirements of the television medium, it attempts to mix comedy-sketch writing devices with identifiable and believable characters. It is a difficult form to play, and not all actors are successful at it.

The sitcom-style commercial is also difficult to play. It, too, is a hybrid. It attempts to give the viewer all the information that a spokesperson could deliver, but in a dramatic format in which the characters appear believable. And remember, the commercial, like the half-hour program, is intended to entertain.

In order to play a slice-of-life scene in this style well, actors must have a few more tricks up their sleeve. We've seen how the characters represent the potential consumer and the product, and we know that the tone of the material must be kept light. Even though these scenes will have all the usual slice-of-life characteristics, they almost always follow this structured formula:

- *Beginning:* The first beat has two to four lines which give you all the acting clues you'll get from the script. These few lines present the buyer's problem and, many times, set up the event—a confrontation between characters, for example.

- *Middle:* The middle beats feature the event—most of the time a series of questions from the buyer and the answers from the seller. This sequence generally leads to the demonstration.

- *End:* As a result of the demonstration, there is a resolution to the problem and/or confrontation and, therefore, a change in the buyer. The sitcom scene usually ends with a little joke or piece of fun banter.

Most of the lines of dialogue are in the middle section, with the entire script spending maybe a total of ten words to flesh out the characters. Look once again at the Steve and Barb scene on page 72. These are the words that establish the given circumstances or describe the characters: *Steve, Barb, hon, late, night school, new husband, pro at laundry.* Compared to some others, this writer has been lavish.

The audition directions for these scripts have remained the same for decades. You will more than likely hear one or more of the following directions:

"They have a good relationship."
"They really like each other."
"They banter or kid with each other all the time."
"Keep it nice and real and conversational."
"Have fun with it."

Yet nothing written in the script can help you communicate these ideas. Therefore, you must demonstrate behavior that makes the audience believe those things are true. There are some very specific things you can do to help you create the impressions you need to create in these spots. Here are some tips to remember as you prepare your audition. First, let's deal with the character of the buyer.

The Buyer

If you are auditioning for the buyer, you must understand some important elements of his or her character. First, your state of being at the beginning is one that can be physicalized. The character's emotional and physical condition results from what we might call "lack of the product": a cold, feelings of insecurity, a headache, loneliness, sore feet—to name but a very few. Your behavior demonstrates the problem that will be solved. The feeling-state with which you start the scene is the feeling-state that is changed by the demonstration. So be sure to let the physical life modify and change in the response to the discovery. It's generally the direct opposite of the opening state.

Next, plan when and where in the script you are going to use and/or discover the product. It must happen *on* a line of dialogue; otherwise, the tempo will slow to a standstill while we wait for you to eat, drink, smell, or touch the product.

The tempo of this style is comedic. Pick up those cues. It must move!

The Seller

The seller is the character who controls the tone of the script. If you are auditioning for this role, you can only bring one feeling or emotional state into the script: a loving acceptance of the poor buyer's predicament. The buyer's problem is no problem to you, and you can handle any skepticism on the buyer's part with quiet, good humor.

Because the seller controls the tone, the actor playing that role must soften anything that seems harsh or too confrontational. This is the tough one. There are a great many events in these scenes that are confrontations. Though it makes for drama, if "Proctor & Gamble hostility" (as one director called it) is played realistically, the characters don't stay nice. Remember Steve and Barb? They might be having their first marital spat if we took what was on the page at face value.

Thankfully, there is a trick to help you soften lines that have too much edge. It's called the *bubble*.

The idea of the bubble was given to me at a voice-over audition. I remember the session vividly. There was one line, "Buzz off, buster!" that I couldn't quite read in the light and fun manner desired. The casting director told me I could fix the problem by dropping the line on a "bubble" of laughter. Eureka! It worked like gangbusters.

Try it. Say, "Buzz off, buster!" Now start a little laugh on the breath and drop "Buzz off, buster!" right on the breath. Suddenly, what was initially a serious warning becomes a fun little reproof. I realized that the bubble was a marvelous device for solving the same kinds of problems in my on-camera auditions. This vocal quality, with its hints of laughter and fun, erases the harshness of the actual words. I have treasured the bubble ever since, and it has saved my neck more times than I care to remember.

If you have Steve put a bubble on the line "Wives! All I need is Nu-Day," it is no longer a defensive whine but a loving tease that simply expresses his "no problem" attitude.

Lastly, the actor portraying the seller must make appropriate physical contact with the buyer as early in the scene as possible. As we have said, this caring contact helps establish warmth and a sense of relationship.

Tips for Buyers and Sellers

In the sitcom-style scene, all the actors should realize that there must be no "dead air" between the lines. Cues must be picked up. It does not mean that you will rush the interior of the line itself, but it does mean that one line butts up against the other. This is a situation comedy: the pace should reflect that.

THE BUTTON

The button is an expression that I believe has its roots in vaudeville comedy sketches. An act didn't seem complete if the actors didn't button or end their scene. The button is a gesture or an improvised line that punctuates a scene and lets us know it's over. The button should arise easily out of the circum-stances. Buttons are short and, ideally, fun. Going back to Steve and Barb, let's look at how that scene might be buttoned. Remember, the person who does not have the last line is responsible for it. That means that Steve has the responsibility in this script.

```
Steve: Guess you got yourself a new detergent.
Barb: Guess you got yourself a new job.
Steve (improvised): [Thanks] or [Oops] or [No
    Problem!]
```

THE SLICE-OF-LIFE AUDITION

Although actors expect scene-playing in commercials to be easy, it can be among the toughest to audition for. These auditions involve reading cue cards, handling props, moving physically, relating to a partner, creating a character, and setting and maintaining an acting style. All these elements must be handled without substantial rehearsal.

Outside the audition room, you should make as many decisions as possible about what you are going to do and how you are going to do it. Analyzing carefully, preplanning, and making smart decisions are your job outside the audition room. However, do not set line readings. Let the words happen as the result of your thinking. If you wish to run lines for cues, that's fine—but don't feel forced to memorize the lines. Knowing your cues and, more impor-tantly, the sequence of the actions should give you enough knowledge of the words so that you won't feel glued to the cue card.

Scenes are no different from all commercials in the concentration and focus that they demand, but sometimes it feels like you're expected to do the impossible. Good homework and strong choices are the key. Work hard in the waiting room—and then stay open to what happens in the moment once inside the studio. Respond to and work off of your partner as much as his or her talent will allow. At the same time, never abandon what you know you must do to make the words work. And always remember that the name of the game is play-acting, with the emphasis on the *play*.

13

Shakespeare and the Spokesperson

In the passages you read, take out all the periods and commas. They keep you from speaking naturally; make your own punctuation.

STELLA ADLER

Androgynous spokes—that's what I call the other kind of spokesperson copy, those commercials that are all about "you," meaning the viewer/listener. There's no mistaking these scripts. The copy might be as complex as that found printed below a picture of a new computer in a magazine advertisement, and the operative pronouns are "you," "your," and "yours" (unlike the character spokes copy that stresses the first-person pronouns "I," "me," and "mine").

Androgynous spokes is the only commercial form that is not primarily about the speaker's feelings. Instead, this kind of commercial text is about information. The person who is speaking is only a means to an end. "Who am I?"—the first thing actors consider when approaching dramatic material—is never a concern in this form. In most cases, with the exception of scripts created for a particular celebrity, the individuality and personality of the speaker only get in the way. I call this form androgynous because speakers have no individual identity; anyone of either sex could deliver the message—even a neuter-gender computer voice could do it.

What the advertiser wants is a delivery that clearly communicates the facts. As the purveyor of important data, your fundamental consideration must be how you can deliver the information to the viewer/listener most effectively. You will be expected to make the copy intelligible to the ear of the listener while creating the impression of a conversation.

CONVERSATIONAL VS. PRESENTATIONAL SPEECH

"Be conversational." Actors hear this simple direction more often than any other in commercial auditions. Unfortunately, it is also the most often misunderstood. I know it baffled me for a long time. That actors receive this note so often suggests that "being conversational" has come to mean a speech that is different and affected, rather than speech that is natural and familiar. I think the phrase first came into use as an easy way for casting directors to tell actors to stop projecting their voices theatrically and instead to communicate over real space. Now I believe the phrase's meaning has expanded to express a casting director's desire for a very "real" delivery. This means the actor's body language and spoken language should be the same as they'd be in the circumstances of everyday life.

This direction becomes a problem when actors confuse natural and real communication with a kind of skewed version of theatrical behavior, particularly as it applies to speech. Many actors flatten their voices and take on a monotone, "ahs" and "uhms" sprout up throughout their speech, and pauses appear in the most unlikely places. I like to describe this attempt at being conversational as actors mimicking something they think the Actors' Studio taught. Needless to say, it does not accomplish the task. But, quite frankly, it's not necessarily the actor's fault.

Attention to our spoken language is not high on our nation's list of educational priorities. In elementary schools, any emphasis on spoken language is reserved for reading aloud, and in the later grades, the correction of speech deficits. Courses in oral interpretation and public speaking, as well as the presentation of one's ideas and personality through verbal expression, are not a big part of most schools' curriculums. More disheartening, many students' speech deficits are overlooked.

Not only is spoken language neglected in schools and universities, but often it is not a major component in the training of American actors. You might think actor-training programs would be different, but my experience with hundreds of actors from training programs all over the country leads me to believe that these skills get short shrift there as well.

Speech impediments are the most obvious vocal problems that are ignored. Tight, misplaced, and unsupported vocal tones get little attention also. What is worse, lots of actors seem flustered at the sound of their own voices, yet no one practices reading aloud anymore. Is it any wonder that auditions and cold readings prove problematical? And the rudimentary idea that written and spoken language are very different boggles many actors' minds.

Given this state of affairs, it's not strange that when actors have to speak conversationally, on cue, they don't know what that means. Contrast this situation with aspiring singers. They spend a great part of their training learning how their vocal instrument works and how to get the most from it. They learn how to read music and understand and use its subtleties. They practice almost every day. The average aspiring actor spends little or no time in similar pursuits. Actors don't see the voice as a crucial part of their acting equipment or a knowledge of spoken language as important—unless, of course, they get cast in one of Shakespeare's plays.

It is no surprise, therefore, that most actors auditioning for commercials feel even less pressure to hone voice and language skills as part of their necessary training. Actors working in voice-overs will be aware of the value of such skills, but on-camera actors (and most of their teachers) pay little or no attention to them. Yet, ironically, these skills are crucial if an actor is going to offer casting directors an intelligent—and conversational—delivery of commercial copy.

You will find that the spokesperson scripts we are about to discuss provide the toughest challenge to actors who are directed to deliver them in a conversational manner. However, if you practice and master the repertoire of skills I describe in this chapter, you will find your spokesperson delivery substantially improved. These skills should also help your work in industrial films and other commercial script forms. They may even benefit your Shakespeare.

The dictionary defines *conversation* with words like informal, intimate, and spontaneous. A conversation conveys information differently from a presentation. Presentations are formal, less intimate and, in most instances, preplanned. The differences between conversational and presentational speech are the differences between the language of friendly peers who share information and the language of an authority who gives information. There are differences in vocal and physical behavior that mark each communication that a listener recognizes and responds to immediately. By mastering the major vocal and physical differences between these two kinds of communication, an actor will then be equipped to deliver any copy exactly the way the casting director desires.

Conversational Speakers

Here are some general observations we can make about the conversational speakers you'll encounter in commercials. Since there is far more physical life in the conversation than there is in the presentation, the *posture* of the body is relaxed and able to respond to the emotional state of the speaker. The body shows little or no tension and always moves in order to express the speaker's feelings. The *hands* are active, not quiet, clenched, or hanging at the side of the body. They move in response to the spoken ideas and feelings. *Gestures* are a response to a desire to express feelings more than a desire to emphasize facts.

The *face* is alive and animated. It responds quickly and spontaneously to the speaker's thoughts and feelings. If that means that the speaker is going to smile frequently, that's fine—as long as the smile is the result of a feeling.

Also, the actor's *costume* is appropriate to the character and the circumstances given in the script. Bikinis to bustles—and all the stops in between—are possibilities.

A conversational speaker's vocal qualities are completely different from those used by the actor delivering a presentational performance. The primary characteristics are:

1. The tone of the voice is the natural tone of the speaker. It might be high and tight, or low and mellow. It is what it is.

2. The tone is utterly responsive to the emotional state of the speaker. Sometimes it makes a liar of the words. We've all heard someone answer the

question, "How are you?" with "I'm fine," when the "I'm fine" is spoken with a whine or downward gliding tone. This person is not fine, and you know it.

3. Conversational English is often spoken quickly. The more urgent the message, the more quickly we are liable to speak. The pace is a function of the feeling.

4. The speech is highly inflected. The inflection is light and at times lilting. Inflection and tone tell us a great deal about what the character is feeling.

5. In real life a conversational speaker's voice might not be supported very well. Whereas performers should always have a well-supported tone, for the conversational commercial they should use their everyday voices, in which their articulation is soft.

Presentational Speakers

Again, presentational speech, the language of the authority figure—the judge, the politician, the teacher, the parent—contrasts sharply with conversational speech. It is the transmitter of important information. The speaker talks to you and expects you to listen and cooperate. It is definitely not sociable or intimate. It is a vocal and physical language that lets you know that no answer is required or expected. Presentational speech is a type of communication behavior that allows the listener to focus on the facts, not the speaker's feelings; it's designed to diminish the leakage of emotional clues from the body and voice.

Speakers we perceive to have authority look and sound a specific and recognizable way. These are the important physical characteristics. If standing, the speaker's *posture* is straight and centered. It doesn't lean in or to one side. It doesn't slouch. If seated, the speaker's back is still straight. The body doesn't slump, lean, or bend over a desk or table. The body is relatively relaxed and quiet.

When the speaker is standing, his or her *hands* rest easily in front of the body and at belt level. They don't hang at the side of the body or over the speaker's crotch. They are never clasped behind the speaker's back. Men may put one hand in their trouser pocket. Physical *gestures* are specific and made to emphasize factual points. They come from the center of the body. Gestures are not a result of feelings; in body language, physical quiet means strength and mastery.

The *face* is not overly animated. It is, if anything, calm in appearance. The speaker does not smile a lot. The speaker may smile, but not too often.

In commercials, the speaker is usually costumed and accessorized in a conservative manner: a suit, a blazer and skirt, simple jewelry, classic hair styling and makeup. With the exception of a wedding ring, men do not wear jewelry. Nothing should shout "look at me." It distracts from the message.

These are the essential vocal characteristics of a speaker we perceive has authority:

1. The vocal tone is slightly lower than it is in everyday life, and it is well-supported. The articulation should be clear but not overly precise.

2. The pace of the language is slower. Pace is a function of the listener's ability to hear over distance and of how important the speaker feels an idea is.

3. Although the voice has inflection, it is less inflected than language with great feeling content. The inflection is more weighty than in real life.

There are many gradations of delivery between the two extremes of purely conversational and purely presentational. As I have said, once the differences between these communications are understood and mastered, the actor can mix and match the elements to create the impression that's required. For example, if a casting director suggests you deliver the copy with "more authority," you can easily create an illusion of having more authority by straightening and quieting down the body, dropping the vocal pitch, taking some smiles out, and keeping gestures in the middle of your body.

Sometimes, your auditors will want to see a "warm" authority. If you are asked to give this kind of delivery, retain your bodily authority, but let the face be more animated. Smile. Lighten your inflection and pick up the pace just a bit. Soften your articulation. Here we are mixing components of each delivery.

At other calls, you'll be asked for a conversational delivery with "just a touch of authority." This happens a great deal with women. The necessary adjustment is primarily physical. Centering the body, straightening the spine, and dropping the chin will probably do the trick. Keeping the gestures originating from the center of the body will also help. Here we have a spokesperson that mixes traits—the body of the authority figure with the voice, face, and language of a conversational friend.

VOICE, THE FOUNDATION OF SPEECH

In the world of commercials and industrial films, the "friendly, warm voice" helps create the illusion of conversation, especially when the material is informational. This friendly voice should not be confused with the gorgeous vocal tone of the announcer of days gone by.

The traditionally soothing, friendly voice has two specific characteristics. First, it has oral resonation and forms a rounded tone that has the warmest vocal quality. You might think of it as the mid-range voice. Second, the voice is focused forward. Think of focusing your speech right behind the upper lip. The rule of thumb is: "Think forward and speak forward." This may sound a little like a singing direction, but high baritones and some sopranos have trouble with this. Their singing training has focused their singing voices in the mask where bone surrounds the resonating chambers. When that placement is held over into the speaking voice, there can be a sharpness in the tone that can cause problems when they attempt a warm, friendly commercial delivery.

As you might expect, vocal problems, such as breathiness, nasality, and pharyngeal resonation, can spell difficulty for the potential on-camera spokesperson.

As you become more familiar with both character and androgynous spokesperson copy, remember that while the intent, the bodily expression, and the "sound" of their language may be different, the language itself is not different. Language is an agreed-upon and organized system of symbols which communicates ideas and feelings. The individual written symbols on this page, for example, are clumped into groups that we recognize as words. These words have specific, mutually agreed-upon meanings. These words are then combined into sentences. Sentences structure the words into an expression of an idea which is larger and more complex than the individual word.

But the actor, particularly the actor in commercials, needs to remember that there *are* two different languages. One is spoken, and one is written. First, human beings acquired spoken language. (In fact, sound as expression came first, then we formed the sound into more specific words.) Subsequently, societies advanced and created written language in an attempt to mirror the spoken language in graphic symbols.

In the transition from speaking to writing, components of the spoken language were left behind. The use of tone, pitch, or pace could not be indicated by the Egyptian hieroglyphics writer, the medieval monk, or the modern-day typesetter. We have been taught to recognize a system of capital and small letters, punctuation marks, and line arrangements as organizational markers which tell us the shape and specifics of a thought. This is the skill of reading. Reading silently communicates to the mind through what we see. Once we start to read aloud and want someone to hear and understand what we have read, we need to use vocal markers in a way that organizes thoughts for the listener's brain through what he or she hears, since all the visual markers are gone.

What are these vocal markers? What are the organizing principles of our spoken language? Actors get into trouble if they don't understand these principles, especially when confronted with androgynous spokes copy. Once you understand how your everyday speech does its job, and learn how to employ that knowledge, you will be able to master this kind of material.

Breath

Speech is organized by the breath. The ruling idea is: "One thought equals one breath." If you want to test the validity of this central concept, listen to yourself. Speak the following two sentences aloud:

```
I'm very interested in environmental issues.
Are you interested in them?
```

You take a breath and begin to exhale and make sound, then you put all the words of the first statement on that breath. You then pause, take a second small breath, and put the words of the question on the new breath.

Now say the words aloud, but breathe after "environmental," and don't pause after issues. This might be written as follows:

```
I'm very interested in environmental.
Issues are you interested in them?
```

This clearly demonstrates how breathing in the wrong place makes the spoken thought unintelligible to the ear. At what point you breathe in a group of words helps define the thought for your listener's ear. As you can see, the typographical symbols marking the beginning and end of the breathing pattern are a capital letter at the start of a sentence and the period and question mark at the end. Only the original sample statement and question use written punctuation to intelligently organize the spoken thought.

Blending

What happens to the words between the capital letter and the end punctuation is what I call *blending*. The sentence organizes the individual words into a larger thought through the use of the breath. One emotional thought is one breath. The words are the details.

Think of it this way: The breath, which organizes the thought, is like a string on which are strung the individual words of the thought, like beads. The beads on this string, however, don't have any knots between them. They touch one another. The end sound of each word blends into the beginning sound of the next word. When the blending stops, the listener's ear knows something about the shape of the thought. Here is the sample, written the way it's spoken. To hear it, I need no spaces between the words.

```
I'mveryinterestedinenviromentalissues.
Areyouinterestedinthem?
```

This is one of the major ways that spoken and written language differ. When writing, we separate the words but enclose the words of one idea within the capitals and punctuation, and the reader's eye can see that. When speaking, we enclose the words of the idea within one exhaled line of breath, and the listener's ear can hear that.

The consonant sounds of our language make this possible. The majority of them are called *continuing* consonants—meaning the breath continues through the sound which allows the end sound of a word to continue into the next word. The *plosive* consonants, of which there are six, require the breath to be stopped in order make the sound. Try to say the sound of an "L," an "M," or an "N" without moving the breath. Nothing happens.

This blending concept is a powerful one, and for the actor in commercials it is positively magical. Blending is the key to a conversational delivery. The softer the articulation of final consonant sounds, and the more the words blend, the more conversational you sound. The more you isolate and emphasize words, the more artificial you sound.

Because you don't communicate ideas on the words, you can't base your acting on them. You do communicate ideas on the breath, which has tone and, therefore, the life-blood of your feelings. The sound of the voice is the emotional thought. But my teaching experience has shown me that actors in androgynous spokesperson copy tend to abandon their natural vocal blending in favor of word acting. Getting them back to natural vocal behavior goes a long way toward helping them achieve a competitive performance.

Blending's power lies in its simplicity, though it demands practice when you first start blending words on purpose. One way you might help yourself become comfortable with this skill is to read into a tape recorder, one paragraph at a time. Play it back to yourself and listen to how much you are blending the words. Practice letting the words melt into each other.

You might also want to use the ideas of breathing and blending in your favorite Shakespeare monologues. Once again, take advantage of the tape recorder so you can hear the good effect these ideas have on the intelligence and conversational quality of his language. Remember, the plays were written more to be spoken than read.

Our next step is to take these basic concepts of breathing and blending and use them as the basis for creating spoken intelligence out of the written presentation.

SCORING

Androgynous spokesperson scripts prove problematic not only because they are informational, but because of the way they are literally written on the page. I often imagine ad agency copywriters, sitting alone in their offices, stopwatches in hand, reading aloud the copy they are struggling to polish. They have an idea in their heads about the thought structures and rhythms they want to hear. They struggle to convey their clients' ideas by the words they choose, the way they lay out the lines on the page, and the punctuation marks they use—or don't use. They are attempting to impress the eye of their most important reader—their client. They focus on manipulating the words and language to communicate their clients' messages. They have time and, in some cases, legal constraints to consider. Their writing must satisfy many requirements before it ever gets into the hands of us actors.

When it becomes our assignment to make this material sound conversational, we may have to restructure—or notate—what is on the page. I call this restructuring *scoring*. Many successful voice-over performers use some version of scoring, a kind of notation that organizes the written words of the script into speakable, audible thoughts. The goal of scoring is to maximize the intelligence of the copy for the ear of the listener. It attempts to mirror what people really do with words when they speak.

I try to think of the words as notes and work to arrange them into speakable melodies. First, I read and evaluate the script in terms of its ideas. Then I notate the page to remind me of how I have organized the thoughts. Next, I look at the punctuation on the page, and think about the inflection and the pacing the ideas demand. The notation serves as my vocal road map.

End Punctuation

The first step in scoring spokes copy is to look at all the end punctuation in the script. Does it really end a complete thought? If it doesn't, be prepared to get rid of it. Read the following lines:

```
Acid indigestion sufferers.
All antacids are not alike.
```

The first two lines of this commercial function as the "attention-getter." But if your goal is to sound conversational, you can't talk in headlines. Since those first three words are not a complete thought, you can get rid of the period, and create a full thought by blending the words right up to "alike." To then mark that this as the end of an idea, place a double bar (//) at the end of the idea. This marks the place to breathe. Now the line should read,

```
Acid indigestion sufferers all antacids are not
    alike.//
```

The next line in this copy features the happy dot trick.

```
Di-Aid is different . . .
```

One of the favorite punctuation devices of copywriters is the *ellipsis,* or three periods (. . .). Usually an ellipsis marks the absence of material. But what it means in commercial copy changes from piece to piece. There don't seem to be any rules. Therefore, be careful—dots pop up all over the place.

In this case, the ellipsis means that the speaker should come to a full stop. It's a complete thought, as well as the most important idea in the script. So for speaking purposes, get rid of the dots, stop, and breathe. You would write the notated line as follows:

```
Di-Aid is different//
```

By scoring copy like this sample, you replace inappropriately written end punctuation with vocal punctuation that makes sense to the listener. I wonder whether the writer noticed that the last sound of this thought was one of the six plosive consonant sounds— B, P, T, D, G, and K. You have to stop the breath to make these sounds. To continue the idea, you must soften the "T" to blend it into the next word. Pronouncing it fully draws focus to the idea.

Internal Punctuation

Next, I score all the internal punctuation: commas, dots, dashes, and any other invention that might occur within a sentence. They represent small pauses in the breath which tell us something about the shape of the thought. Some of the punctuation will correspond to the patterns of oral speech, and some will not.

Once again, get rid of any internal punctuation that does not help communicate the ideas to your listeners in a way they are used to hearing, and strike anything that does not help you make auditory sense of the script. For example, written and oral communication show an obvious difference when it comes to commas in series. In grammar school, we were taught to put commas between words and phrases in a series:

```
Please buy some milk, bread, butter, and cheese.
```

Writers must use commas because what speakers actually do when saying a list can't be put on paper. When we speak, we differentiate the items not by commas, but by changing our vocal inflection for each item. Instead of commas, perhaps a better way of symbolizing on paper the slight rise and contrasting fall in the vocal pitch of each word would be to insert arrows pointing up or down through those words:

```
Please buy some milk, bread, butter, and cheese.
```

Vocalizing the written punctuation in a series is a fast way of letting an agent or casting director know that you are not good with this type of commercial material. They know it doesn't sound right. They don't know why, they just know.

Another way we use commas in writing is to set off amplifying information within the full thought. The heart of the thought is the subject and predicate (verb + object). In one way or another, everything else describes or amplifies them. Whenever describing information comes before or between the subject and verb, it is set off by written commas—for example:

```
In these complex times, your current tax service
    may be letting you down.
```

"In these complex times" is a word group that amplifies the thought by providing the context of the idea: when the event may occur. It comes before the subject—"your current tax service"—and the predicate—"may be letting you down." Consequently, the written comma is vocally indicated. Likewise, commas or pauses would have to be made audible if that phrase happened in this position:

```
Your current tax service, in these complex
    times, may be letting you down.
```

However, no spoken pause would be necessary if that phrase came after the subject and predicate:

```
Your current accounting service may be letting
    you down in these complex times.
```

Although using these guidelines will help you *say* rather than *read* the copy, always test the intelligence, the *shape*, of the thought in your ear. Eliminate and/or add pauses based upon what you want your listener to hear and understand. And of course, be sure to blend the words between all the pauses.

INFLECTION

A speaker draws a listener's attention to specific details, or words, within a thought by changing the pitch of the voice, or the inflection, which accents these words. That's how we clarify our thoughts for the listener's ear. An upward, or rising, inflection is the automatic first choice of the speaker.

Normal conversational English is quite inflected. In commercials, you should keep inflection light in order to achieve a performance that will be deemed conversational. The voice goes up, touches the word, drops back, and moves on. The pitch change is not extreme—just a slight lift. Avoid a monotone; it may be a character choice, but it is not a model of average speech.

Blending is the handmaiden of the conversational inflection. If you are isolating and, therefore, hitting, leaning on, or elongating words, you will not be able to create the illusion of conversation.

Inflection helps you accent the important details in a thought. The question is, how do you know which are the important details? Well, once you have organized the thoughts in a script and scored the pattern of breathing, you will have a good idea of what the material is about. One sure way to check yourself is to create a little *precis,* or condensation, of the spot. Use the product name and words from the script to write one simple sentence that expresses the core idea. This will really help you know exactly what the spot is about. If you find your sentence becoming too long or complex, you'll know that you're off the track. Strive for simplicity. Copywriters don't have time to deal with many ideas—especially not complex ones—in 28 seconds. Generally, they are only writing about one major copy point.

Once the subject of the commercial is established—telephones, antacids, or cake mixes—everything else becomes a description that expands our vision of the product—"easy," "delicious," "quick"—of what the product does, and of how to use it—"just one wipe," "helps protect," "whisks you right through." These are the details you want your listener to hear.

Here are some examples of the use of inflection to make the specific idea about the product clear to your listener's ear. Again, I have used arrows to score the lifts in vocal pitch.

The Ho↑liday Sale at Sears (not any sale—the *Holiday* Sale)

TWA Bu↑siness Class (not first class, but *Business* Class)

Send the ve↑ry best. (not the best, the *very* best)

Just ↑one wipe . . . (just one, not two)

medicated formula that helps pro↑tect . . . (not soothe, but *protect*)

Whi↑sks you right through . . . (not helps you, but *whisks* you)

Notice that the word that follows the inflected word stands out to your ear because its pitch contrasts with the previous sound. That contrast is achieved by lightly touching on the inflection, then dropping off and back to the tonal line.

In conveying any thought, your inflection will change according to the point you wish to make. That point will depend on the surrounding structure of ideas. Be sure you know what you want the audience to hear. Is it:

    ⬆
    Extra-strength Bufferin

or is it:

                         ⬆
    Extra-strength Bufferin

or is it:

                ⬆
    Extra-strength Bufferin

It is important to remember that sometimes the detail that needs to be heard occurs at the end of the sentence, as in the line, "Di-Aid is different." By marking the inflection, you will not be tempted to give in to the downward intonation glide that naturally occurs at the end of a spoken statement.

                        ⬆
    Di-Aid is different//

There is a trick to learning how to accomplish inflection with this light and seemingly spontaneous quality. The secret is located in your index finger.

If you ever watch actors in voice-over auditions or recording sessions, you'll be struck by how much they use their bodies, particularly their hands, during the performance. The connection between the fine motor coordination of our hands and our speech is undeniable. I can prove it by using my index finger as a baton to direct my voice's pitch change.

Use your arrows as guideposts to show you where to lift or "pop" your finger. This is a small, simple flicking motion, just popping up your index finger as if you were conducting a flea-sized orchestra. When the arrow goes up, your finger goes up. You'll notice that the higher you lift your finger, the higher your pitch will go. It allows you to accomplish inflection without even thinking about it. It is a great skill to have on the set when everyone wants a different reading of a line and you have no time to practice.

The fine motor coordination that connects your voice and your index finger is the root of the gesture. The coordinating of the breath/tone and your finger is a result of the impulse to communicate.

You'll notice that androgynous spokesperson copy has lots of imperatives, or commands. These scripts love to tell the listeners or viewers what to do: "Try it," "Taste it," "Look," "Compare," "See," "Think." Experience tells me that when I'm asked for a conversational delivery, these commands can be made into "friendly" commands by putting them on an up inflection.

"And" and Others

A word of caution about the word "and." Inflecting "and" inappropriately is another way of showing an agent or casting director that you don't have your skills together. "And" is one of the few words that change meaning if it is put on an upward inflection. When used as a simple conjunction which joins fairly equal ideas: "The soup is quick and easy"—it remains uninflected; the "and" is not important. It functions as a simple plus sign in arithmetic. But if I inflect "and," I change its meaning to "in addition" or "furthermore." The words on either side become unequal, and it is implied that the idea that follows the inflected "and" is the more important of the two.

Many readings have been fouled up by the actor's habit of inflecting every "and." Writers have been so disappointed in our ability to speak the language that they might write the above line like this: "The soup is quick 'n' easy."

Another caution concerns the inflection of personal pronouns such as "I," "me," "mine," "you," and "yours." As with "and," actors seem to want to make these words important in every position and in every commercial they are asked to read. Be very sure not to inflect these pronouns unless they really have something specific to add to the thought. That occurs in comparisons: "My eyeliner is better than yours." It does not necessarily happen in a simple statement: "My eyeliner is brown." When you are just starting out, be very sure to inflect these pronouns only if you have a very good reason.

PACE

Pace is an important element in spoken communication. We tend to slow down phrases we think are very important. It is as if the more important we think something is, the more slowly we say it. Notice that I didn't say we slow down a word; I said phrases—groups of words. What we do is slow down a mini-thought within the larger thought. This slowed-down phrase was called "a hundred-dollar bill" by a voice-over teacher that I once knew. He gave it that name so that his students would remember how valuable a tool it is for making a point. He also liked that term because he wanted them to spend them sparingly in a piece of copy. His guideline was no more than three to a script.

Let's look at some phrases within larger thoughts that might benefit from a retarded pace. Slow the bracketed phrases in these lines of copy:

```
The New Spacemaker II is big enough to take [a
     full sixteen-inch casserole].

[Better arthritis pain relief], that's the
     Medivil guarantee.

Look...[visible tartar must be scraped off]. But
     you can fight cavities and tartar [between
     check-ups] with Tartar Control Fresh-Up.
```

These phrases attract the attention of our ears because they are surrounded by a normal, conversational pace. Pay attention to blending, even though the pace is slower. Breathing and blending are always your first considerations.

ACTING

Now that I have described the technical aspects and challenges of this copy, the only thing left is the vocal tone, which is a function of the acting. As spokespersons we are not dramatizing the material, but in order to be conversational we do need to have a feeling point of view about what we are saying. The clues to that point of view are found in the copy or in an emotional idea associated with its subject. An emotional idea connected with good food, for example, is love.

Your clues in the copy are the operative words, the words that describe or the phrases that come up two, three, or more times and enhance the subject—words like "easy," "powerful," "fast," "safe," "smooth," or "soft." They convey an emotional idea and, therefore, suggest the vocal tone that the script needs.

Let's say the operative word is "easy." I am going to choose an acting adjustment that produces a light vocal sound and a "no-problem" interpretation; or I might choose an action like "sharing great news." Unless the casting director wants a very authoritative reading, I would avoid such doings as teaching and convincing. Nine times out of ten those choices make the speaker too harsh and preachy.

Many product groups are constantly associated with the same emotional idea. These are the feelings that the clients like to have attached to their products. Here are a few:

Good Food

This includes cereals, bread, soups, and so on. These nutritious, wholesome foods use advertisements whose subtext is always about love. The person who chooses or prepares or serves good food is always loving and warm. The preparation and serving of these products is an expression of their caring.

Fast Food and Snacks

The subject of these spots include microwave popcorn, junk food, fast food restaurants, and prepared foods like TV dinners. They are essentially about fun or service or making your life easier. You always have a wonderful time while you're enjoying these food products.

Cleaning Products

These always have an element of being "easy" and a feeling that it is "no problem" to use them. After all, what person is going to buy a bathroom cleaner that implies it will make the job harder?

Beer

The tone of beer ads varies depending on whether they are foreign or domestic and whom the brewer has designated as their predetermined audience. It can range from fun to adventure to victory and power.

Banks and Financial Institutions
Nine times out of ten, the underlying feeling has to be one of trust and stability. No one wants to put money into an institution that seems sleazy or shaky.

SUMMARY OF COMMERCIAL TECHNIQUE
The challenge of androgynous spokes and other commercial copy is a creative one. You are in charge. You control everything regarding what the audience perceives. This demands thinking and practice and is not mastered in a day. But even in the beginning, your intelligent use of the techniques we've discussed in the previous chapters should garner you noticeable results.

I'll bet that the amount of concentration and skill necessary to work in filmed commercials surprises you. It's not a craft for the faint-hearted. I've given you a great deal to think about, and I wouldn't be surprised if you were feeling overwhelmed. But remember: One step at a time. I don't believe in quick fixes, and neither should you. These techniques will take time to assimilate into your personal acting process. Don't attempt to get it all at once. Go back, read a chapter slowly and carefully. Write in the margins of this book, think about the ideas, even try out the techniques in your other acting work. And experiment. There is a lot of information here, but it all boils down to a few ideas and concepts.

For all the words and exercises, the techniques that I've been discussing find their roots in some very simple verities. The first is the power of *doing*. Not pretending to do, *really* doing. If you have trouble understanding what an acting teacher means when he or she says you aren't committed, it only means you weren't really doing the tasks (think of the Nike commercial and "Just Do It").

Put the focus outside yourself. Concentrate on the circumstances, your partner, the message or point—on anything except yourself. Once you get yourself out of the mix, you have an opportunity to start to act. When you are the focus of your thoughts, it's impossible to become enmeshed in the imaginary life of the script and your character. It blocks your ability to imagine and invent, two processes at the heart of your work. A student in my film program made the following observation:

> I'm finally getting it. If I hear that little inner voice commenting while I'm doing the scene, it means I'm not in the moment. In fact, it means the moment has already passed me by.

Next, trust the mind–body connection. The body knows every nuance of behavior necessary to communicate the mind's ideas and feelings, and the mind reads every sensation of the body as it interprets and forms an understanding of the world around it. The two cannot exist without each other, so trust in this miracle of interdependence. It will work for you all the time. All you need to do is keep the instrument in good working order.

Use your intelligence. Engage and involve your mind in your work. The more you seek to understand the material you're working with, the more likely you are to give an audition that you can be proud of. Treating a piece of copy as if it is "just" a commercial, or hoping that "winging it" is the way to keep it alive and spontaneous, will not do you much good. Evaluate the script, decide what you want to do with it and why. Use your insight to understand its logic. Before you work, really think about it, but then let go—never think about the work while you're doing it.

Finally, be brave. You must give up trying to control the moment. Choice implies risk, but you must make a choice. The choice may be "wrong." Do it anyway. Have the courage to be wrong. Stop trying to please, and you'll start doing more interesting work. Release your tensions and let your impulses have their way with you. Release, and you'll be surprised how quickly the imagination starts to invent.

To put this even more simply, focus, think, and be brave in the moment of doing. Let go of the outcome and respond in the moment. You will know you've got it when it feels a little like flying. You will own it then.

Break a leg!

Part Four
GETTING BOOKED

14

Unexploded Landmines

What you don't know can *hurt you!*
ANONYMOUS

You may wonder why I've put a chapter called "Unexploded Landmines" in the section of the book that deals with getting bookings. The reason is that many actors out in the auditioning world of commercials, and other auditioning worlds, are carrying with them habits that are potentially lethal to their success. They are doing things personally and/or in performance that hamper their ability to fulfill acting assignments or communicate effectively with the people who may represent or hire them. I hope you are not one of them.

Almost all these habits can be minimized or eradicated. But before that can happen individual actors must come to grips with what is really going on with them. The problem, in my experience, is that too many "wannabe" actors are unwilling to seek out good advice and listen to it. They pay good teachers a lot of money, and then fail to heed what they say. One of the great gifts of working in a good on-camera class is that if such actors don't believe what the teacher says, maybe they'll believe what the camera *shows*.

Unexploded landmines fall into three categories: physical, vocal, and psychological. The first two are easily seen and heard on-camera. The third makes itself known in acting choices and interaction with teachers, agents, and casting directors in particular. If you have a problem in one of these areas, you have probably been told about it. The question is, did you pay attention? Much of this assumes that you are in—or have been in—a safe learning environment with sensitive and insightful instructors.

PHYSICAL LANDMINES

Let's start with the body. Have you been told during an acting class or in a note during a show that you need to "loosen up" or that you are "too tight"? If you've been told this more than three times, you had better pay attention. This condition will not go away by itself.

Here are some questions for you to think about and answer for yourself as honestly as you can. If you don't know the answers, pay attention to yourself and find out.

- When your are standing listening to your partner in a scene, does all your weight go onto one leg?

- Do you get tension headaches because you are carrying your chin in the air?

- Are you able to stand still, be emotionalized and deliver your lines?

- When you gesture, is all the motion starting at the elbow (so that your look like you have chicken wings)?

- Do you continually bend into the camera or your scene partner when you are delivering your lines?

- When you are standing waiting to begin, where are your hands? Are they behind you, over your crotch, or hanging by your sides?

- Do you need to be doing an activity to feel connected—that is, able to connect with an emotional state?

- Have you been told in a camera class or audition to leave your face alone?

- In a camera class, have you been told that you move your head too much?

Physical tension—tightness—means that your instrument is out of tune. In our discussions of technique in earlier chapters, we stressed the importance of an instrument that can resonate with the behavior needed to communicate the subtleties of the mind. Too often in the training of American actors, the body, the mind's instrument, is left to fend for itself. Actors are counseled that they need "body work," but put it off or deem it not that important and/or too expensive. Their sense-memory work makes them feel like they're acting, while body work lacks glamour, so the latter is ignored. For those whose personal history has led them to a greater physical tension than others, that is a mistake.

No matter what you do, if you do not address the alignment of the body and the release and control of tension, it will affect your ability to be wonderful. It will affect the way you sit in a chair and walk in a room.

Do something about it! The Alexander technique, the Williamson technique, and yoga practice are but a few of the ways to get in touch with your body and allow it to be your friend and creative collaborator.

The body also includes the eyes. If you can't see the copy, you can't read it. Needless to say, if you need glasses, get them, and if you don't look good in glasses, get contact lenses.

One other problem surfaces in the commercial class. It not only stops actors cold in commercials but will impact upon all the auditions in which they have to read from a "side" or script: It's what I call "the old cue card problem"—the inability of the eyes to function together for quick and accurate focusing. This means that when you are reading a cue card and you take your eyes away from the card and go to the lens, and then attempt to return to the card, you will—or fear you will—lose your place. We all lose our place on the card when we are relatively new at it, but, generally, we overcome the problem fairly quickly. If losing your place persists and you experience the same thing when you read aloud, or you feel you must go back and reread paragraphs when you are reading a book, you may have a visual problem that all the cold reading classes in the world won't cure. You need to seek out a developmental optometrist who can diagnose this "tracking" problem and help you solve it. The good news is that it can be successfully treated, and the cue card and the cold reading will no longer defeat you.

VOCAL LANDMINES

The voice and body are one. Sound is made by the body. Vocal problems are uncomfortable to confront and correct, so actors often try to ignore them. Because the voice is such a psychologically sensitive instrument, scary things can come up while you are attempting to center the breath and find your voice.

The voice—and the speech that it makes—often reflect muscular tension, bad habits, and insecurities of all kinds. Remember, many times vocal tension is caused by not breathing while you are acting. Here are some of the things that can happen as a result of vocal tension:

- You race through dialogue, and the casting director or teacher constantly tells you to slow down.

- Your voice is thin or whispery, so that you cannot be heard.

- You have been asked to have "more vocal presence" in auditions.

- You receive the note to "calm down your face"—meaning that you are thrusting your jaw and opening your mouth unattractively when you speak.

- You are told to lower the vocal pitch or your performance (speak lower).

- You feel out of breath when you are reading long copy or are doing a monologue.

- Your singing teacher tells you that your major problem is one of support or an unreleased jaw.

- You grind your teeth at night and sometimes have pain in your jaw.

- When you are rehearsing a role, you are prone to laryngitis.

- You are told that you have a "covered" tone, particularly if you are a male.

These are some of the comments and experiences that should alert you to the fact that your voice needs attention. This does not mean you need a singing teacher but a skilled voice and speech teacher who will assist you in rebuilding or repairing your vocal instrument. This kind of work costs money, but if your voice is impaired you should invest in your voice instead of staying in an acting class. Prolonged neglect of some of these problems will not only hurt your acting, but can be dangerous to your health.

PSYCHOLOGICAL LANDMINES

These are the tough questions! Becoming aware of how we behave should help us understand the behavior of others, and an examination of *ourselves* becomes the focus of many acting classes. As inappropriate as I feel that is, I do believe that actors must come to grips with how they present themselves. This is an extremely personal business. Careers are built on "likeability." Everyone knows everyone else, and they talk to each other.

The very nature of the business causes stress and affects the stability of most of us. Actors are constantly competing for roles—an audition is a competition. And in the commercial world, you could be competing two to three times a day. Rejection is the norm, acceptance the unexpected. The struggle to meet and acquire an agent, impress the right casting director, and stay focused when you not only want the job but need it, tests self-esteem and forms a seed-bed for hostility. You, and only you, can monitor your response to these realities, and only you can take the actions necessary to cope with them.

Attitude, arrogance, and anger are the trilogy of trouble. None of them serve the average actor well. Attitude and arrogance are the ones that agents and casting directors mention first on their lists of what turns them off in actors. There is a difference between quiet confidence and "blowing your own horn." The actor who lets everyone know that he or she "knows" how things should be done, or announces to an agent that he or she is the next Tom Cruise or Julia Roberts is asking to be dismissed. Humility and manners are valued greatly. Being able to connect honestly with another person and talk about things other than the business, is vital to the "good interview."

Anger takes its toll in very real ways. We all have our anger in our lives, but too often I have seen actors use the difficulties of the business to fuel their personal ire. It infects their professional relationships and, many times, their acting choices.

The demonstrated opposite of this trilogy is the lack of self-esteem, which can be as damaging as overabundant confidence. It is also destructive to your development as an actor. Even if you're not confident in life, you must be confident in your work.

Your best friends probably won't tell you, so how can you know if you need to do some personality adjustment? These are not all the questions that you might investigate, but they are a beginning:

- Do you believe that there is a small group of actors that get all the work, and that that's the reason it's so hard to break in?

- In agent interviews, do you talk primarily about yourself and what you have done?

- When you are redirected in a class or an audition, do you attempt to explain what you were doing?

- Do you ask for an opinion (for instance, about your headshots) and then proceed to argue or tell the other person what you intend to do anyway?

- Do you apologize not only for your work but for a host of other things that occur?

- Do you feel that evaluations made in class or notes given by directors have personal overtones?

- Do you remember people and something personal about them?

- Do you know all the things that are not right in a situation, as opposed to some of the things that are?

- When is the last time you genuinely thanked someone?

- When is the last time you did something for someone in the business without tying it to a professional reward?

Success in any aspect of the acting world is like playing comedy: the ending is happy, but the work is demanding and difficult. It isn't an easy way to make a living. It demands talent and a whole lot more. It demands discipline of body and mind. You are the only thing you have to work with. Listen to those whose insights you trust, be honest with yourself, and have the courage to change.

15

Being Ready

Auditioning is the work; work is the perk.
                        GIDEON Y. SCHEIN

Actors audition for a living. There is no better way to describe how professional actors spend their time. The ones who are always working are always
auditioning. Even stars frequently find that it goes with the territory. Actors
who do not audition well have a very serious problem. It is a problem they
had better address, because no one in show business will be patient with it.

In no other performance medium do actors audition more frequently than
in commercials. Every actor's goal is to be sent out on lots of auditions. Busy
actors in New York or Los Angeles might expect five or six auditions a week,
if business is good. As we've noted, far more commercials are produced than
feature films, so this number of auditions is possible—and desirable.

Auditions do not always lead to employment. That sounds obvious, but
many actors can't accept the reality that there are good actors who go to a
hundred auditions before they book a job.

THE WORK OF AUDITIONING
Turning opportunities into employment is the primary reason to work at auditioning skills. The tragedy is that years are spent training the actor's instrument, and, in most cases, little or none of that time is spent learning how to
use it under pressure, when it really counts.

Acting teachers are not necessarily the best audition teachers. They are
process-oriented, as they should be. Audition coaches have to be result-oriented. They need to understand the acting process and help the actor apply a
shorthand version of it to the audition material. They are not primarily concerned with teaching acting. They have one goal in mind: getting actors to
use their training in the moment of truth, when the super-objective is to get
the job. They are concerned with their students' ability to show up emotionally and deliver the goods under the worst of circumstances. Good audition
teachers are worth their weight in gold.

Auditioning is extremely unnatural. You are asked to walk into a room full
of total strangers who will judge you and to give them a solid and emotional-

ized performance while remaining relaxed and open to changing it. Your ability to pay the rent next month may depend on their positive evaluation of you and your work, but you're not supposed to let that rattle you. Obviously, anyone who indulges in this kind of self-inflicted stress is harmlessly but mildly demented!

The first fact you must deal with as an actor is that auditioning is not a comfortable way to make a living. You really have to want to be an actor more than anything else in the world to participate in such a ritual. There is nothing wrong with you if you suffer anxiety in this process; everyone does to a greater or lesser degree, and you wouldn't be human if you didn't.

In the competition that is auditioning, one person wins and everybody else loses. A competition means that your skills are being matched against those of others. You have to want to win, while understanding that there is nothing personal in losing. If you lose, you'll live to compete another day.

Auditions are desired, and also feared, opportunities to display your gifts, where you exercise your control, or you feel under the control of others. The audition itself has got to be dealt with as an event over which you can have some measure of power. It has got to be thought about and talked about. It must be discussed not in terms of "How do I get an audition?" but in terms of what you need to do to be ready so that you are capable of making the most of this unique type of job interview.

Working in this medium today is serious work. It isn't something that you can dabble in. You have to acquire knowledge not only about your art but also about the business. We all know that serendipity plays a part in life's most important endeavors, but preparation and practice are the keys to winning the prize.

I could do a whole book on what preparation means, but you might not listen to me if I told you: "Don't audition until you are ready." I have been asked repeatedly by my students to explain what I mean by "ready."

As apparently random as audition success may be, there are real and concrete things you can do to load the dice in your favor. Three essential parts of your audition preparation should be *presentation, skills,* and *attitude.* Let's examine the first two of these here, and consider the issue of attitude in Chapter 16, where we discuss your meetings with people in the business.

PRESENTATION

Presentation is the way you physically present yourself and your credentials to the industry. You'll recall that in the character spokesperson chapter I said the most important question you can ask is *Why.* Well, it's the first question you should ask yourself about yourself. Why should anyone hire you? I'm sure you're attractive and adorable, and in your university or professional training program or local community theater group, you are considered a talented performer. But so are lots of other people. Your first task is to appraise yourself with some objectivity.

That's a hard thing for an actor to do, but in commercials it's really vital. If you don't know what you have to sell, no one else will. And if you are not aware of how much more you can develop your skills, your personal growth as a performer will be stunted. Work with yourself to discover, value, and exercise your strengths while simultaneously uncovering, minimizing, and correcting your weaknesses. Review Chapter 14 and consider what unexploded landmines may pose obstacles to your success.

Type

Sanford Meisner said that the marketplace will tell you what it wants from you. Look at commercials, and look at print ads. Advertisers will generally hire actors with the same look and style as those appearing in the product's or service's print ad when they begin their television campaign. Study the faces you see in both. Is your face there? Avoid fashion magazines in this exercise—those faces are generally going to be the beautiful young people working in the modeling industry. Instead, look at ads in magazines like *Good Housekeeping, Time, Woman's Day,* and *Newsweek.* This is nuts and bolts advertising. Follow the same distinction when you are watching TV. Most of the actors in the hair, makeup, and perfume commercials, for instance, are models, but elsewhere, what you should see are a range of types and ages. Are you in the cereal commercial where the girl talks about health and the outdoors? Are you in the bank behind the customer-relations desk? Are you the truck driver, the delivery guy, or the hairstylist? Find faces that look like yours.

Also look at the situations in which those faces find themselves. That will help you decide if you are the mom, the blue-collar worker, or the upscale professional. Look at how those actors are styled. What clothes and accessories are they wearing, and how is their hair done? You can then match yourself against their image and get hints about audition wardrobe and hairstyles. This homework will give you an idea of how the industry will see you and, quite possibly, cast you.

What we're doing in this exercise is what we did with the acting ideas: embracing the stereotype. This is one of the hardest steps to take and one at which actors falter. They fight the fact that they can't play everything, moaning about the business being so shallow because it is preoccupied with people's appearance. This reality makes some actors angry, and so they fight its truths. Finding your identifiable type is the first step toward knowing what you should present at an audition.

Once you've identified your type, in both face and body, and examined all the details and styling that surrounds it—hair, clothes, makeup, jewelry— once again, be honest. Do the young moms in the commercials you see have hair down to the middle of their backs? How many men on TV have full beards? Are there actors working steadily in commercials that have unsightly moles, crooked teeth, recognizably bleached hair? Do the women have dangling earrings? Do the men wear earrings?

As real as commercial characters are meant to be, the physical presentation of the actors you see is generic and slightly idealized.

Remember, commercial images have to be accepted and understood by an enormous viewing public, and the people who do the hiring need you to be identifiable to that public. That does not mean that the commercial world is only about white, blond, and bland—it isn't anymore. Advertisers need all kinds and colors of actors in commercials today, but only idealized versions of those kinds and colors.

Once you've made your informed decision about yourself, you can start to get your "look" together. If you are serious about the business, get rid of the things that might provide prospective employers with a reason for not hiring you. Fix anything that bothers you—your teeth, for example. Indulge in one good outfit that is in keeping with your type: jeans and a pressed shirt for the blue-collar guy; a suit and tie for the fellow who looks like those corporate types. Khakis are perfect for the upscale casual guy. Be sure that the colors flatter you and the patterns don't draw focus away from your face. You're not trying to create a costume but a socially presentable and flattering outfit that hints at what you can play. Invest in a good hairstyle (that goes for men *and* women), and well-applied, appropriate makeup (no high glosses, please). Embrace the stereotype.

SKILLS

So now you think you're ready to get headshots, right? Wrong! While doing the homework suggested above, you should also get yourself into an on-camera training program of some kind. If you live in or close to a good-sized city or a well-equipped school, choose a class that is suitable in level to your acting background. If you don't have that luxury, look for camera exposure in any legitimate setting you can find. It will give you an opportunity to check your look on camera to see if it matches your vocal sound and acting quality. You'll also have an opportunity to experience "real space" projection (see Chapter 6).

Most of all, an on-camera class will be a place to hear and see what you need to do before you go to the next step. Do you need to loosen up in an improv situation? Does your speech need tending to? If you're studying acting, keep studying acting. If you're not studying acting, start. Don't get those photos until you are satisfied that you know what you have to sell and have acquired your skills.

Especially acting skills. Today's market is about actors. That doesn't mean that novices aren't being sent to auditions. These talented beginners are generally quite young and have some kind of background, like modeling, for example. It does mean that agents are looking to represent people who know something about the craft. The important thing is that your auditors will be more interested in you if you've studied with reputable teachers and have some performance experience. This experience could have been acquired in your university.

HEADSHOTS

Armed with a clear vision of yourself and where you fit into the casting picture and with a growing collection of performance skills, now you are ready to get some headshots.

This is not the place to save money. Ask as many people and look at as many photos as you can until you can make a list of photographers whose work you like. Then interview these prospective photographers. Choose one on the basis of his or her past work and how you feel about that person. You have to click with this person (no pun intended) if you are going to get the best pictures possible.

A good headshot for the commercial market generally is one with a smile. That may vary according to your look, but keep in mind that generally the tone of the messages you'll be delivering in commercials is upbeat. There should be a sharpness of focus to the picture so that the eyes are crisp and clear. And there should be a connection between the eyes and the smile.

There should be contrast between the background and the person. Clothes should be your own and should help strengthen idea of type. Varying shades and interesting patterns in your clothing help create subtle interest and avoid a flat quality. Hair and clothing should be styled to frame the face which is the focal point of the shot.

The critical questions are: Does the picture look like you at your best? Does the person in the picture project a personality? Does the picture help to place you in an identifiable casting niche?

Price should not be the deciding factor. If you are serious in your plan to be a working professional, you have saved and budgeted for start-up costs. You are your own business, and you must be prepared to make an investment in it. Scrimping on pictures is penny-wise and dollar-foolish. After all, your headshots are your business cards.

Be aware that the average life of a headshot is two years; then it probably should be replaced. It's what you're going to present to strangers as a representation of you and your talent. Everything about your pictures, résumés, postcards, and any other business communication should be absolutely top of the line. If you can't put your best foot forward in this presentation, how can anyone expect you to put your best foot forward in the audition?

You never get a second chance to make a first impression. Emblazon that truth on your bathroom mirror as a rule you must never forget. You are embarking on a career that is full of first impressions. The casting directors and agents that are your lifeline to work are paid to remember actors. They are paid to remember a name, a face, and a quality. If you send them a picture of you that is badly lit, poorly reproduced, and shows you in a deeply dramatic and somber pose, you can bet your life that they will remember not to remember. Getting your presentation together takes time, thought, and money.

Résumés

The back of your headshot should be covered by your résumé. It should be firmly attached, not paper-clipped or stapled in one corner. If you can, get it printed on the back of your pictures.

Your résumé is an organized list of your skills and the projects you have professionally done—in sum, all the things that communicate that you are ready to audition and are right for the job.

Aside from your name, the most important thing on your résumé is your contact number. The next are your union affiliations, if you have them. If you are a union member the next thing you need to list is your Social Security number. Casting directors need that in order to check your union status.

If you have a great deal of experience, customize your résumé and create one for theater and one for film and television. Organize your theatrical credits by starting at the highest level—Broadway first, for example, then off-Broadway and regional theater, then summer stock, and so on, in descending order. Director's and star's names help identify a production you were in; these are people you worked with, after all. Your film and television résumé should deal with credits in the same order, beginning with any feature-film work, of course. Work you have done as an extra in film and television does not belong on your résumé.

Beginners should not despair. Their résumés should feature their theatrical training, student films, and special skills. Unless you are from a very well known and respected university training program like Yale's, the professional world does not care about who your college-level teachers were, but they do care about who your professional teachers and coaches are. The good news is that being a beginner is a positive thing in the world of commercials. You are a new face, and that is always a strength.

Professional or beginner should avoid cluttering the résumé simply to have a full page. Clarity about the things that speak to your proven abilities or your investment in and commitment to a professional career are what count. Never list a special skill in which you are only marginal in performance. If you claim to ride a western saddle, you had really better be able to ride it well. If you claim to drive a car, state whether it is a stick-shift or automatic, and be sure you have a valid license. A valid passport is another document that can sometimes make hiring you more attractive. Commercials are shot all over the world, and you could book a job that will be shot in Rome and have to leave the country three days from now.

Finally: *Never ever lie on your résumé.* This is a very small world in which everybody knows everybody else. No matter how little you have done or where you did it, the truth is always best. Everyone had to start somewhere.

Contacting Agents

Once you have your presentation together, the first people you'll need to contact and meet are the talent agents. Unfortunately, commercials are a part of show business that preclude getting much work without agents, so you are going to need to clear another hurdle and obtain agent representation. This is a task made necessary by the speed with which everything is done.

Casting directors usually don't get breakdowns, which describe what kinds of actors are needed to fill the roles in commercials, until one or two days before the casting session takes place. Most often, casting is one of the last preproduction jobs. In most cases, the session is "prepped" the day before the audition date. Prepping a session means that the casting director for the commercial talks to agents and decides who among the agent's clients will get an appointment.

The casting director rarely has an opportunity to go through picture files in order to find new faces for a session. In the main, he or she lets the agent do the scouting. This short-cutting is why it has become customary for agents to get you commercial auditions on a regular basis. An agent's job is to establish an ongoing relationship with casting directors, with the result that the agent gets called upon for the prepping sessions.

The object of your initial presentation and mailings will be to impress those agents. Your local area's agents are for you to find. Call your local Screen Actors Guild (SAG) or American Federation of Television and Radio Artists (AFTRA) office for a current list of franchised agents. Also, there are seminars and workshops in every major market that will give you specific tips on the way your local market functions.

Mailings

When you have your skills, presentation, pictures, and résumés ready, it is time to do your first mailing. Mailings are now the traditional way to contact agents, for they do not want to be telephoned; agents already spend a lot of time on the phone with casting directors to get breakdowns and appointment times for their clients. Dropping by without an appointment is a definite No-No.

Your first mailing should consist of your 8 x 10-inch headshot with appropriately attached résumé, plus a cover letter attached to the front of your picture. The letter itself should be on professional-looking stationery no larger than 5 x 7 inches, and it should have your name printed on it. Type your letter unless you have impeccable handwriting.

Writing cover letters takes some practice. Let the agent know as concisely as possible what you want—that you're requesting an interview, for example. Agents know you are looking for representation and work. Refer to your résumé and point out a recent show, booking, or completion of a professional training program. If someone the agent knows has said it is okay to use his or her name in the text of your introduction, do so—and do not do so if you do not have permission. Stay respectful in how you close the letter and avoid the temptation to be clever or cute.

The agents to whom you mail your queries is a question of where you are. In the smaller markets, there will not be many agents to contact, so you are best to mail to all of them. Get the name of the person within the agency to whom you wish your mailing to go. In smaller markets, investigate production companies that may do their own casting.

In the larger markets, there are professional guides such as the *Ross Reports,* in New York, which list all the agencies, their personnel, plus casting directors and ad agencies. You can find these guides in bookstores that specialize in theater literature and at many newstands in the theater district. Do not mail to all the offices listed. Instead, carefully check the legends that identify the agencies that handle commercials and get the names of the agents within those agencies who are directly responsible for that kind of work. Choose one agent in each agency to concentrate upon. Your rule of thumb in a major market would be to identify ten to twelve agents.

You can do a major mailing to as many casting directors as you wish.

Do not expect to get an instant answer to your mailing. Agents, like everyone in the business, get backed up and sometimes do not have time to look at each day's mail as it arrives. Maintain contact by sending a postcard-résumé—that is, a postcard with your headshot, name, and contact phone number on the front of it. I recommend that your postcard photo be the same as that on your 8 x 10. You are attempting to build face and name recognition, and changing to a different picture on your postcard does not accomplish this. Two pictures on the postcard may communicate that you can present two genuinely different appearances, and that can be to your advantage, but if you do not have two very distinct looks, avoid this device. Send your postcard every two weeks for two months and then send it every four weeks religiously. Send only to your targeted group of agents and casting directors. Do not feel the necessity to fill the other side of the card with information. Avoid being cute and only say hello, unless you have done something or booked something. Then let them know it.

Continue this for a minimum of eight months before you target another agent in the agency and begin again. Michael Shurtleff sent postcards to Broadway producer David Merrick every week for fourteen months before he got an appointment and, consequently, the job. Persistence counts.

This method of contact must also be maintained after you have meet with an agent or casting director. Do not assume that once they have met you, your name and face will fly to the forefront of their minds with every breakdown they receive. They have many clients and meet numerous new faces every week. "Postcarding" them after your meeting, every two weeks, and then every four, will build name and face recognition and help them remember you, your résumé, and what a pleasant meeting they had with you.

Some closing words of caution: Do not send a thank-you note to a professional contact and include your postcard. If you think they won't remember your name without a picture, then you shouldn't send the note. The same is true of Christmas cards. Do not include your postcard—that's tacky. If they don't know you or remember you, they will not mind not being overlooked in your holiday mailing.

16

Interviews and Auditions

You never get a second chance to make a first impression

ANONYMOUS

The mailing has gotten you an appointment with an agent. Now what? Meeting an agent is probably going to be your first "audition." The agent doesn't have the power to give you a job, but he or she does have the power to get you to the people who can.

Some agents will ask you to read copy. Some will not. In most cases, the response you are going to receive from an agent is going to be based on your presentation and the personal chemistry between you. Chemistry plays a large role in the relationships in your professional career.

ATTITUDE

In Chapter 15 I said that addressing the issue of your *attitude* was one of the three essential elements of preparation for working. Acting is a personal business, so the attitude you bring into meetings, especially interviews, is very important to the outcome. Many times, attitudes are everything. They supersede talent as the deciding factor in who gets the job. The sooner you become conscious of the "vibes" you bring into a room, and the sooner you pay attention to your social skills as well as your acting skills, the better you will do.

Begin to structure your business attitude with an important premise: Casting directors, agents, assistant directors, directors, account supervisors, and everyone else you may meet in the business are *people*. Generally, they are nice people. Sanford Meisner's good advice is: "Get your focus off yourself"—get it onto the people with whom you're dealing. They are real people with real feelings. They get very tired of everyone wanting something from them all the time. They have pressures and problems and lovers and bosses.

Positive people who listen and respond appropriately get their attention. Agents and casting directors are not interested in representing actors who are bitter, defensive, overly pushy, or brash. Thus you should not bring your personal "baggage" into any business meeting or audition. Agents have neither the time for, nor the interest in, hearing the reasons why you may have been late, why your pictures aren't good, or why you feel life is treating you so badly. You shouldn't be looking for a sympathetic parental figure, you should be looking for a business partner. That's what *they're* looking for.

Listen to what they have to say—both the positive and the negative. If it is positive, great; if it isn't, don't fight, justify, or deny what they have to say. Listen and evaluate. There is nothing more infuriating to an agent than someone coming for help and advice who responds to a comment like, "I think you would do much better with your hair shorter" by retorting, "I need it long for my theater work." If I were the agent I'd respond to that by advising the actor to pursue theater work, then, and not see me again until he or she is serious about commercials. A bad first impression! A better answer would have been. "You really think so? I'll look into it." The actor can make whatever decision he or she wishes without negating the advice of the person who is trying to help by sharing an expert opinion.

Manners count. Many of us are a little too casual and insensitive in our business dealings these days. For instance, don't assume you have the right to address people by their first name until you have been introduced and given permission. There is a pertinent story about the great casting director Shirley Rich: When a young actor, upon meeting her, called her by her first name, she responded, "Ms. Rich to you." She bristled at the young man who was so lacking in courtesy as to call her Shirley without permission. Never presume familiarity with professionals who outclass you in experience, knowledge, and, most likely, wisdom about the business. Besides, this is a hard business, and anything that adds a little graciousness and respect to it is of value. "Please" and "thank you" are dignified expressions of caring. Respectful communication is the name of the game, so being nice reflects well on you. Everyone wants to help that "nice young actor" they just met. They have little interest in helping the young actor who has neglected the "manners part" of his or her presentation.

Agents are truly keen on meeting talented people with a marketable look ("good packaging") and a strong knowledge of what they can do. Most of all, they want people who can book the job. They want talent that's easy to work with, and not desperate. Remember the trilogy of trouble in the Chapter 14: Be aware of your own attitude, avoid arrogance, and make adjustments where feelings of anger can trip you up in a meeting.

THE AUDITION

Now—praise the gods!—everything has gone well, the agent has called, and you have a real audition for a real commercial—tomorrow. Beside the name of the product and where you have to go to audition, ask the agent if he or she has an idea of what "they" want. Agents are more than happy to give you all the information they have. That might include everything from the wardrobe requirements for the audition to the shooting dates planned for the spot. Write it all down.

For the audition, embrace the stereotype as much as you can without getting in a full costume mode. Little things make a big difference: glasses, a tie, a shirt open at the collar, hair pulled back, a blazer as opposed to a T-shirt. Dressing the part is becoming more and more necessary in the audition. Have an audition wardrobe that is always ready to go at a moment's notice. As you add to it, keep color, line, and design in mind. If you don't know about these things, invest in getting the information.

Arrive dressed and early, especially if you have been told that there is loads of copy. Every audition will have a sign-in sheet of some kind—a list you sign when you're ready to audition. If you sign it right away, before you are ready, the casting director may come out of the studio and call you in before you've had adequate time with the material. So I advise you to do your homework while you wait. Spend your time with your script. Lots of actors have fouled up auditions because they spend their time in the waiting room chatting. What's worse, they've spent their time in the waiting room bitching about one thing or another. (Attitude again.) The mindset to get into right before you go in for the audition performance should be upbeat. (See the check sheet at the end of this chapter.)

Remember, you don't want to practice specific line readings, or try to memorize the entire piece. If you say the material aloud, you may freeze the reading in your ear and brain and tend to make it difficult to accommodate any changes that the casting director may give you. Just know your first line. This will make it easier for you to enter the frame from your "moment before."

Always make sure you know the correct pronunciation of the name of the product. If you've been watching TV, you should already be aware that words like "ibuprofen" need to be added to your vocabulary.

Set a goal for yourself in the audition. If you make the goal of each audition getting the job, you'll likely fail and be frustrated. It is a fact for you, as it is for every actor, that you're going to be rejected far more often than hired. You need to set achievable performance goals for yourself. For example, I remember one student who made it her goal in an audition to look the casting director in the eye. She did it. As a consequence, she left the audition with a feeling of personal accomplishment. She had taken control.

It's important that you decide what you want to work on in the audition process. You are taking back control by making the audition something that you can have impact upon, by not giving all the power over to "them." Each audition is an opportunity to rehearse and learn something else about yourself and/or the work.

If you allow the audition to become a matter of life and death, if getting the job is the way you continually measure your abilities, be prepared to lose confidence in those abilities in a very short time. The need for realism is the reason that I and other teachers who work with auditioning actors encourage them to audition for everything they can. Does it mean they want every one of those jobs? No, it means they've got to get on their feet as much as possible in front of strangers and practice delivering a solid presentation of their acting skills. Practicing your preparation, goal-setting, and performance skills every chance you get, whether you want the job or not, will strengthen your ability to audition well when it really matters. Auditioning is a skill in itself, perfected through knowledge and practice.

PERFORMANCE ANXIETY

Maybe the greatest benefit of focusing on a personal audition goal is that it helps the actor deal with the ever-present performance anxiety. We all have it. The question is: Does it use you, or do you use it?

The stress of an audition creates an unavoidable response in the human organism. It is called the flight-or-fight reaction to fear. Our bodies are deluged with adrenaline, and our lungs want to hold on to as much oxygen as they possibly can. Our primitive selves get ready to kill that woolly mammoth or run away from it. But we can't kill the casting director, and we can't get the part if we run away.

The only way to deal with this primal response is to take control of it. One way to do that is to breathe: Deep, controlled breathing lets your mind know that the mammoth is really a mouse. This should be the time that all the work in your vocal production class and the release work in your movement class pays off. If breathing exercises are good enough for corporate stress-management classes, they should be good enough for you.

You can't think, let alone feel anything except panic, when you are in the grip of fear. All the fancy talk about centering is really talk about getting consciously controlled breathing in place. Logic and preparation can then follow. For the actor who suffers from extreme performance anxiety, more may be required. An excellent book on performance anxiety, *Fearless Presenting,* by Eric Maisel, Ph.D., describes many calming and control-taking techniques available. Some form of psychotherapy may be helpful. Be careful that you do this work with professionals in that field, not with acting teachers.

DEALING WITH CASTING DIRECTORS

The basic rules we discussed in reference to agents pertain also to casting directors. Let's hope you are the actor who is the answer to their prayers. They want you to be wonderful. As we said earlier, treat them as real people, listen, ask intelligent questions, and do the best you can that day. Don't make your time in the studio with them all about "love me, love me." They don't want to marry you; they only want to love the performance you can put on their tape. As partners, you and casting directors have a job to do, and they don't have time for anything else. Their focus is on producing a casting tape that their client will think is excellent.

If do you get the job, a polite note of thanks is appreciated. It isn't necessary to shower gifts on casting directors (or agents). It smacks of bribery. Be realistic in this area. If you have a long-standing relationship with someone in the business and want to give him or her a Christmas gift, that's fine, but don't do it for everyone you know. With casting directors be very selective. I've only given a gift to a casting director once—a special little goody from Rome where I went on a job she had cast me in.

CALLBACKS

When the audition is over, leave. Don't linger and try to find out how you did. You will probably only get feedback on your audition from your agent—and only if you did poorly. Otherwise, you'll get a callback or hear nothing.

Of course, the goal of the auditioning actor in commercials is a high call-back ratio—a good number of callbacks for the number of auditions. If your agent is submitting you correctly, and you are delivering consistently good performances, you should be running at least a 50-percent ratio of callbacks to first calls. Does this mean that you will book 50 percent of those auditions? No, it means that you and your agent are doing your jobs well.

The callback is another audition, but full of unexpected elements—all bets are off after the first time you came in. This time the copy may be different; the direction may be different; you may be asked to audition for a different part. With luck, the director will be there and be the one who gives you instructions on what he or she wants to see. Just listen. Stay as open and flexible as you possibly can. Don't worry that it's not the same as last time, but attempt to give them what they are asking for now. Enjoy the experiment.

Those of you who receive lots of callbacks will, quite logically, be the ones who are most often passed over in the final rounds of casting, and for lots of reasons. Maybe they decided to go with a different look or age, or the director didn't feel that the right chemistry existed between you.

Your attitudes in the callback are crucial. Remember, one of your goals in this business is to attain a reputation of being easy to work with. This is not the place to argue, put the blame for your performance deficiencies on the copy, or otherwise prove yourself difficult to work with. The small margin of control you have in an audition is over yourself and the way you handle the material.

All audition experiences are not nice. Some can be downright difficult. There can be stresses and strains among the creative team that have nothing to do with you. The director may not be a "nice guy." Keep your focus on your work and not on the forces that may be swirling around you—that's how you'll avoid being swept up in them or taking the experience personally.

And try to train yourself to leave the audition experience behind you after you go out the door. If you set a goal for yourself, you'll know if you have accomplished it or not. Praise yourself if you did and take possession of a job well done. Try not to mind-read the other players who were in the room, and by all means don't spend the residual money until the check arrives.

No matter what they have said about your performance at the callback, forget it. It's a well-known maxim that the more praise you get at the time of the audition, the less likely you are to book the job. Kudos you receive in the room are called "the kiss of death." Leave the audition and go on with your life. Try not to worry. You did your work as well as you could. Or, if you feel you didn't, find someone to show you how to do it better.

An Audition Journal

The audition is a journey of discovery and self-mastery, a process that will challenge you to become better than you are. Even if you lose the booking, you gain if you did your job correctly. Even though you may not have gotten cast, you will have learned something about the business and yourself.

I encourage you to keep an audition journal in which you record all your auditions for all kinds of roles. Write down what you auditioned for, when, for whom, and who sent you. More importantly, record your feelings and perceptions concerning what happened, both good and bad. Try to pinpoint where you may have dropped the ball. What was the critical technical skill that failed? What one didn't? What was said to you? What do you wish you had said? It is critical that you be as honest as possible about what really happened. Write about all the thoughts, ideas, and feelings you had during the audition process.

This is one of the ways to discover and defuse those unexploded land-mines we've talked about. Did you prepare? Did you prepare well? Were you dressed correctly and comfortably? What really gave you anxiety or put you at ease in the waiting room?

Read the entries every couple of weeks and try to detect patterns that will emerge. If you have been told more than once to slow down, you'll know you need to pay attention to your tension level and your breathing. If you have been told more than once that you need to show more energy or be more conversational, you'll have a clue as to what work you need to do—so that you don't hear those notes again. The journal is a method of self-exploration that should help you figure out what kinds of additional work you may need to do. Do you need to work on breathing? Do you feel unpretty in your makeup? Do those MOS commercials still make you a basket case?

Using your journal in this way, you will be able to establish meaningful goals for yourself in the audition: skills to be worked on, habits to encourage and continue, habits to get rid of, and successes to be repeated. This process should help you take control of your personal audition growth. It's the diary of your auditioning life.

Best of all, you'll be taking control of what seems uncontrollable. It can be done.

The Audition Checklist

I wrap up this chapter with a helpful step-by-step summary of my technique, and I also suggest how it applies it to the practical aspects of auditioning. It might be a good idea to photocopy this list and take it with you when you go to your next audition:

1. Arrive early and pick up the copy. Do not sign in. Go to a quiet place and read it through quickly. See if there are any surprises and if there are any clues to a specific look.

2. Go to the restroom. Adjust your look if you need to—for example, pin up your hair, take off your tie. Fix your makeup, if need be, and take care of any other last-minute styling concerns. Do some deep breathing if you need to get control of your nerves. When you have yourself physically "together," go back and read the copy again. Do not sign in.

3. Identify the form of the script, which should be apparent from all you learned in Chapter 7. Identify the acting style. Remember that the product demonstration is the key to separating film style from sitcom. The quick test is the question, "Does this character represent the product?" If it doesn't, you know you've got a "Honeymooners"-style script; it's meant to be funny. Once you know the style, you will have the key to the tempo and a good idea of what the spot needs in order to work.

4. If you have a scene, pinpoint the event. Invent one if you have to. Check your five Ws. Come up with simple answers. If you are the character who enters, be sure you know where you're coming from and why. If you are the character who is discovered in the frame at the beginning, be sure you have an appropriate activity. If the scene is about two peers of the same sex, be prepared to play both parts.

5. If the role is a character spokesperson, find the point of the story—what the character wants us to know. Mark out the beats and decide upon your verbal actions. Construct a strong moment before that pushes you into the first moment. Know how the character feels and what he or she enters to do. I guarantee that you'll be directed to be conversational.

6. Be sure to absorb all the information in the script—not just the on-camera lines. Read the voice-over, too; there may be information in those words that will help you understand your story better. If there is a storyboard available (see the Appendix for a sample storyboard), look at and read it carefully. Notice the character's expressions and the body language that the artist depicts. These are great clues to what they expect to see you do.

7. Never spend time saying the words out loud, unless the script is for an androgynous spokesperson. Try them under your breath (sotto voce) and be more focused on cues and content than on how the line sounds. Stay loose—walk the hall if you feel yourself losing energy.

8. If you've got androgynous spokes copy, get out your pencil and start making your road map. Think about the precis of the commercial, and quietly try the thoughts on your ear. Make sure that you have your breathing

under control. You might wish to vocalize a little in the restroom. Once again, get up and walk the hall if you feel yourself losing energy.

9. Set your audition goal.

10. Now that you have fully used the opportunity to familiarize yourself with the script, you are ready to sign in. Because you waited, in order to do your homework, the casting director will not have called you in before you were ready.

11. Greet the casting director with an upbeat hello, go into the room, and go to the mark. Be friendly, but remember this is not the time to network. You are there to do a job.

12. At the end, say goodbye and thank you. Do not comment negatively on your work, even if you thought it was the worst audition of your life. They may have loved it.

13. Go sign out. Go home and write about the audition in your journal.

14. Congratulate yourself on your accomplishment.

17

The Language Barrier

I want lots of eye acting.
      MATTHEW ROLSTON, DIRECTOR

One of the biggest obstacles to great performances in commercials is that actors and the majority of the production team on the other side of the camera do not speak the same artistic language. This is because actors come from theatrical backgrounds and almost everyone else comes from either technical or advertising backgrounds.

Many commercial directors have entered the profession via one of two paths. Following the first, the agency path, hot-shot art directors or whiz-bang producers leave their advertising agency to work in a production company as a "director." The other path is that taken by the gifted still or fashion photographer, whose success leads him or her to cross over into movies and/or commercials. In either case, their backgrounds have not given them much knowledge of the actor's craft or the way actors communicate about it. As in all the various jobs on the other side of the film or video camera, these directors will spend more time and energy mastering the technical requirements of the medium than they'll spend finding out how to successfully coax a great performance from an actor.

The agency-bred directors may have had little experience dealing with "talent"; they come to the creative enterprise of making commercials well-trained to give respond with great sensitivity to their clients. Their clients' demands always receive their primary focus—and rightly so. After all, the clients foot the bills. Therefore, if an advertising agency's concept demands that an actor smoothly deliver 28 seconds of copy without missing a beat while being hydraulically lifted from a prone to a standing position, so be it. The director will solve the technical problems caused by the advertising agency's decision to use that special effect, but may not so easily solve the problems the actor has delivering the lines under those conditions. As much as directors and their clients crave new faces, everyone breathes easier when the talent chosen for the job has lots of experience.

For obvious reasons, still photographers who turn to directing commercials are primarily visual in their approach. However, most of these proven image-makers have worked with people before. Their use of human models in their photographs seems to have sensitized them to the real and imagined needs of the performers who appear before their cameras. Although they are always aware of the client's agenda, this type of commercial director seems sensitive to individual concerns and willing to strive harder to satisfy the needs of the actor in the production. Still, this director's priority will always be the total effect of the images, and is even less prepared to deal with the problems of an actor on the set once the difference in the actor's style of communicating becomes an issue.

A COMMUNICATION GAP

Some directors are known as "dialogue directors" because they supposedly specialize in spots in which the actors have lines. Yet it has been my experience that even these directors are unable to tell me where and how to cut half a second out of my reading. The talent of all these directors lies in their facility in creating the image: pictures that enhance and expand the literal and emotional message of the client. They are brilliant at what they do. However, if the job requires them to get a performance from an actor in addition to a great-looking piece of film, many of them stumble. They don't know how we actors do what we do, and consequently they don't know how to talk to us about it. They might know what they want, what the result should look and sound like, but often they are at a loss if they have to guide actors to it.

Recently, I was hired to coach an actor on the set of an Oil of Olay commercial shoot. The director who hired me was an extraordinarily talented fashion photographer who was making the switch to directing commercials. He was a man of great creativity who left his ego behind as he embarked on a television commercial project that involved beautiful images and wall-to-wall copy. He knew at the callback that the young woman whom he wished to hire wasn't understanding him. But after I talked with the director, it became very clear that he knew exactly what he wanted. The problem was that he and his agency people had unrealistic expectations—they had a staggering list a mile long—of things that they wanted the actress to accomplish in 28 seconds. The performer had two pieces of painfully similar copy. In order to create the pictures that the director wanted, however, the script demanded that she do each piece in its entirety, top to bottom, perfectly for each shot. Along with perfect enunciation and interpretation, they wanted specific movements of her body and hands. And of course, they wanted her delivery to be easy, smooth, and conversational.

In addition to all these demands, the director wanted something he called "eye acting." He told me what he meant by describing a scene in an old Barbara Stanwyck film. It was a powerful visual metaphor, but actors would never understand what the director wanted if they were asked to try "eye acting." I suggested that what he meant was a thought that begins in privacy and is brought up and into the lens at the end, just like the behavior I described in the section on tasting in Chapter 9. Once I understood the visual result he wanted, I knew I could help the actor achieve it.

The communication gap is always exacerbated when the director and the ad agency producers have their ideas about the look and the sound of the desired result frozen in their heads long before the start of the shoot. Translating their vision into actable instructions that will elicit a sense of real behavior and spontaneity can become an insurmountable challenge.

For actors on the set as well as in the audition, the solution is to know how to solve their own problems and not rely on the directors' ability to help. It isn't that the directors don't want to help, it's that they cannot. In commercials, you are there to help them, not the other way around. Live by that idea and your value to this industry will rise. Your ability to translate their "language of result" to the actor's "language of process" is pivotal.

THE LANGUAGE OF CASTING DIRECTORS

Nowhere is this need to translate more crucial than in the commercial audition. Once you understand the material, understanding what the casting director wants from your performance is the next step.

The commercial casting director, like the directors just described, does not always come from a background that acquaints him or her with actor jargon. The roads to their jobs are very diverse: Some have been performers, and some have not, and many have had artistic backgrounds in fields like painting, music, or the decorative arts. The talent of good casting directors seems to grow out of a sensitivity to the arts, and, no matter what their background, casting directors gain insight into an actor's process through their exposure to so many performers. The good ones come to understand and appreciate actors; they empathize with the actor's problems and acknowldegre them as the raw material of their trade.

Speed is as much a problem for the casting director as it is for the actor. The need to audition a hundred people for one role in the course of one day causes tremendous pressure. Casting directors do not have the luxury to spend time with each performer, to try to elicit each actor's best performance. The necessity of moving talent through the casting process as quickly as possible has led them to develop a kind of directorial shorthand. The words and phrases that they use to try to communicate the adjustments they seek in an actor's audition have become the industry's jargon. Many of casting directors have learned the jargon from their predecessors. I doubt whether casting directors even realize how similarly they speak to talent. For the newcomer to commercials, especially one coming from the theater, the jargon can be confusing.

It's confusing because it is about the final product—the "language of result." Casting directors' language describes the look and/or sound of the results they want. When they ask actors to "be conversational," "more authoritative," or "more energized," they are describing what they want the effect of your performance to be—the way they want the audience to feel about what you're doing. It's their description of the illusion they want you to create.

All casting directors are invested in having you do a good job. The casting reel they submit to a director is their résumé for their next job. Or, if they are on staff, a reason for the continued security of their positions. The more good performances they get on that reel, the more they will be judged as having done top-notch work.

The really good casting directors work at finding ways to make the audition more comfortable and, therefore, more successful for the actor. However, the expectations of agencies and directors continue to grow, as does their desire to see more and more people, placing an even greater strain on the lines of communication between actor and casting director.

But despite the clear need for good communication, it has not improved. In fact, the fragmentation of the production process, coupled with agencies' and producers' continual search for the "casting director of the month" with this week's batch of new faces, has led to a diminishing of communication and understanding. And actors are vulnerable to the consequences. Now, more than ever, the actor hears little more than bare-boned clichés that are supposed to serve as direction.

A Casting Language Dictionary

There is little we can do about the problems on the other side of the camera. Our concern is to stay focused on the job to be done. That means that the first thing we need to do is translate the result descriptions into actable ideas. What follows is an alphabetical list of directions that are used in auditions everywhere. Casting directors may use them as part of their introduction before they tape you, or they may offer them as tips for subsequent takes. These directions are also part of the language you'll hear on the set. They translate approximately the same way.

Be conversational. If you hear this from a director, it is essential that you pay special attention to your breathing and blending. You are probably talking individual words rather than blending thought groups. Allow your upper body to be part of the communication. Unlock your hands from in front of your crotch, behind your back, or straight at your sides. Don't forget the moment before. Start with a breathed, feeling sound, and be sure that you're doing something with the words. Lastly, make certain you are communicating over real space.

Bigger. Check that you are playing in the right style. You probably aren't. This note means that they want a larger-than-life character with a strong physical life. It usually implies a comedic approach. In the film or sitcom style, add physical life. Don't get louder.

The character has a sense of humor. You must bring the humor in at the top of the spot. Set it up in the moment before and bring it into the frame with you. If all else fails, get the bubble going in the moment before and come in with that. "Has a sense of humor" generally implies that the character directs the humor at him- or herself. It could be classified as the "Oh!-what-a-silly-goose-I-was" adjustment. A confession of fault makes the character wonderfully human.

Don't act. This direction is given in an attempt to get a naturalistically sized performance for the camera. Communicate over real space and don't overproject vocally. Soften your theater articulation. Let the feelings be made known by behavior. Remember, behavior can be an eye movement or a shrug of a shoulder. Don't indicate. Don't try to convince the camera of anything. When all else fails, "admit" your story to your friend the camera.

Don't push. This is another way to tell you "You're working too hard" (see below). All the notes on that direction apply.

Have fun with it. The character/characters are slightly larger than life, so check that you are playing the correct style. Get rid of dead air between lines and pick up your cues. Find the humor in the writing and play it, or adopt a fun-feeling point of view for your character and play that. Don't be afraid to be too big.

Have more fun with it. Sharpen the character idea and go toward a more comedic stereotype. Comedic tempo is a must. Lastly, try to let go, be loose, and invent in the moment.

Just talk to me. All the ideas encompassed in being conversational (above) apply here. To intensify the feeling that you are really connecting with one person, focus on looking *into* the lens, not *at* the lens. This becomes a real doing, and, although it's subtle, it has an amazing effect upon the audience's positive perceptions of the character.

Loosen up. This one means exactly what it says. Get your hands to the center of your body and involve your upper torso. Don't be afraid to shake yourself out before you start.

More authority. Be physically centered and stand straight. Use your hands from the center of your body. Keep your physical life relatively quiet. When you get this note it probably means that it's the intelligent delivery of the information that should be your first concern. Give your voice oral resonance and speak forward. Check the phrasing of the thoughts, and with your eyes reach right through the camera's lens to the viewing audience.

More energy. Without fail you can address this note by answering the question, "What are you doing with the words?" The commitment to moment-to-moment *doing* always creates the illusion of an energized performance. It is just about guaranteed.

More friendly. Smile! That is one of the friendliest things you can do. Smiling will even make you feel friendlier. Check that your voice is not in the upper part of your register. Drop it into an oral resonation and speak forward. Are your moment-to-moment doings appropriate? Is your chin down? Are your eyes reaching into the camera?

Pull it back. Don't physicalize as much, but be sure to keep the intensity of the thinking. Remain committed to the feelings and doings but let what happens on the outside just happen. Check that you are vocally communicating over real space.

Relax. Breathe—breathe—breathe! You can do nothing if you're not breathing. Don't be afraid to shake yourself out between takes.

Say it one-to-one. This means much the same as "be conversational" (above). It means that the dialogue is naturalistic, and the casting director wants appropriate vocal and physical behavior.

We want it very real. This does not mean that they want a monotone voice and an unenergized read. People are real to one another because they have feelings. Bring strong emotional stakes to a spot when you're directed this way. But don't impose a physical life; rather, let the emotional life "leak" through the voice and the body. That's what happens to real people. Allow yourself to think before you say something. You are not married to the lens, so don't feel obligated to stay eyeball-to-eyeball with it. In the audition, if they "want it very real," you'll be shot in a tighter closeup than usual; therefore, it is crucial that you be aware of the real-space considerations.

Talk to a friend. This is another of the several ways that casting directors tell actors to "be conversational" (above). Always assume that being conversational will be the casting director's first choice for the delivery. If they want something beyond that naturalistic approach, they'll let you know.

Throw it away. This means that you should really soften your articulation. Blend the words. Don't get sloppy—just soften your enunciation, particularly of end consonant sounds. The moment before is vital. Make sure your acting choices come out of the circumstances and are not based on product. Also, don't feel chained to the lens, particularly in this mode or any other "conversational" spot. People do not hold conversations eyeball to eyeball; they look away, they think and talk while fixed on an interior image or an object in the environment. Treat the communication as if it is happening in a small real space. That way, you'll automatically control the size of the vocal and physical expression. Stay super-focused on the feelings and what you're doing with the words.

You're working too hard. This means that it's likely you are not communicating over real space, so vocally—and possibly physically—your performance appears strained. You may be forcing your face to work, rather than letting it respond to the thoughts. You may find that you're trying to make sure the audience "gets it." Drop any notion that you must convince your audience of anything. To put it another way, you may be acting words, instead of expressing thoughts.

These translations are offered to you as guidelines for you to think about and try out. Will you find variations in the interpretation of these pat phrases? Of course! However, my definitions have been tested on hundreds of students and have been heard at thousands of auditions.

Good luck!

Appendix 1:
Sample MOS Commercials

Imagine that you walk into an audition and hear the casting director deliver one of the following commercial scenarios.

A TELEPHONE COMPANY

Female

Your first job away from home. In the city. You have worked late and its raining. You're tired. You're returning home to your brownstone apartment. You open the door and enter the lobby, expecting a letter from home, you go to the mail box, open it and find it empty. You are disappointed. You go to your apartment door—open it—come in, turn on the light. Look around. You are very aware of how empty it is. You really miss your mother—the phone rings and it's she. Line: "Hi, Mom."

Male

You have been waiting for this day for months. Your sailboat was delivered last night and it's on the trailer in the driveway. All of your friends are coming today to help you launch it. You enter, go to the window, open the drapes and discover it's storming outside. No launching. No party. You are extremely disappointed. You look around the room. What are you going to do now? You turn on the TV. It's Saturday—only cartoons. You don't want that! You turn it off. You pick up a magazine. That's not what you want either! You're restless—bored—still unhappy and disappointed. The phone rings. It's your buddies! They're coming anyhow—you'll have the party in the garage.

A VACATION RESORT

Female

You are on a bus into New York for work. The bus is jammed in traffic. You look out the window and realize you're going to be late again. You look up at the sky. It's been raining for three days and the sky is still gray and dull. You think, "I don't want to be here." Where do you want to be? You want to be on a beach under a palm tree by a beautiful blue ocean.

Male

You're on the 59th Street Bridge driving to the Hamptons on Memorial Day weekend. Friday. Traffic is jammed. It's hot. Horns are beeping. Tempers are flaring. You know it's going to be hours before you get where you want to be! You think in exasperation, "I don't want to be here!" Where do you want to be? On a beach under a palm tree by a beautiful blue ocean.

AN INSURANCE COMPANY

Female
Your husband has been in a severe auto accident. You have been at the hospital all day. He will recover, but it will be a long time until he can work again. You enter your kitchen. Turn on the light. It's very late. The dog runs to greet you. You sit down at the kitchen table. You're worried about how you are going to manage to take care of him, the kids, the finances. There is a stack of mail on the table. You decide you must handle it. You open the first envelope. It's the mortgage bill. The second piece of mail is the car payment. The third is the dentist bill. Your concern and worry mount with each bill. The last piece is a letter and a check from his insurance company. The letter states that you will receive the check every week until he is back at work. It will cover your financial needs. You are relieved and grateful.

Male
You're seated at your desk. It's late. You're tired. Your major client has a very serious problem. You are going over documents and trying to find a solution. You discover the solution. You pick up the phone, dial—tell the client his problem is solved.

A CAMERA MOS EXERCISE
This is an MOS that requires personalizing props, using an internal monologue, and working in the playing space in a manner so that you can be seen by the camera.
Enter camera left, cross to desk, pick up coffee, cross to window right—look out of the window, then cross back to the desk—sit and make a phone call.

The goal is to justify the movements by creating your own story. Deal appropriately with the space and camera. Remember that you must cheat to be seen.

Appendix 2:
Sample Slice-of-Life Commercials

The following are practice slice-of-life scenes. One note to the actors: do not read the lines that are assigned to the voice-over (VO). They will be added later.

COOKIES—A MAN AND WOMAN
Two young people sitting around the table late at night.

> Man: You know, these Home Baked Chocolate Chip Cookies taste great. I could eat the whole bag.
> Woman: Mmmm... I can taste the brown sugar.
> Man: Mmmm...I can taste all those chocolate chips.
> Woman: Mmmm...I can taste the eggs. The molasses.
> VO: Home Baked Cookies...so good you can almost taste the recipe.
> Man: I'll give you everything I own for that last Home Baked Cookie.
> Woman: I already have everything you own.

DETERGENT—A MODERN COUPLE
A woman gets ready for work; her husband enters.

> Woman: Hey, Mr. Mom, did you do the laundry Monday?
> Man: Yeah, why?
> Woman: Well you forgot to wash my favorite blouse.
> Man: It looks clean.
> Woman: Hmm? It smelled clean a few days ago.
> VO: That's because with some detergents, your clothes only smell clean for a short time. But Breeze gets clothes so clean...they look clean...they smell clean...and they stay smelling clean till it's time to wear them again.
> *(Time passes)*

Woman (smelling laundry): Mmmm...just washed?
Man: Oh, I washed that last week...with Breeze.
VO: Breeze. The clean smell lasts so you know
     your clothes are really clean.

TRAVELER'S CHECKS—HUSBAND/WIFE/BELLMAN

A couple in a hallway of a hotel, at their room's door.

Husband: Maybe it's my keys...wait a minute, Sue?
     Do you have the cash and travelers checks?
Wife: No.
Husband: No?
Wife: I thought you had them.
Bellman: Is something wrong here?
Wife: We lost all our cash and travelers checks.
Bellman: No problem, there's a Check Express
     refund machine right down the hall.
Husband: But, they weren't Check Express.
Wife: They weren't?
Bellman: Oh...let me think.

DETERGENT—MOTHER/DAUGHTER

The daughter is entering the kitchen from having finished changing the car's oil.

Mom: Ya did it!
Daughter: Just takes know-how, Mom.
Mom: Know how to get a good old-fashioned clean?
     That velour top is dirty.
Daughter: No problem.
Mom: You can get that clean?
Daughter: Old-fashioned clean from a detergent
     with a new-fangled fabric softener.
Mom: Strong 2'll clean this?
Daughter: Plus you'll love the softness from the
     new-fangled fabric softener.
Mom: I'll have to see it, and feel it.
Daughter: Watch.

(A little while later)

Mom: No more tire treads--that's an old-
     fashioned clean.
Daughter: And...?
Mom: Feels downright snuggly.
Daughter: No static cling here.

Mom: I see it and I feel it...That's...
Daughter: Know-how.

FROSTING—SCHOOL TEACHER/PUPIL

This is a cooking school. The teacher, Mrs. Gibbs, finds Nancy making the wrong icing.

Mrs. Gibbs: Nancy, what's this? I told the class
    to make buttercream frosting.
Nancy: It's new Dream Frosting, Mrs. Gibbs.
Mrs. Gibbs: MMM! Creamier than buttercream. MMM!
    Lighter than buttercream.
Nancy (VO): And Dream Frosting's easy. Use
    Instant Pudding--makes it creamier...and
    Whipped Topping Mix--makes it lighter.
Mrs. Gibbs: Nancy!
Nancy: Yes, Mrs. Gibbs?
Mrs. Gibbs: Congratulations! You taught me how
    to make a better frosting.

HOME SECURITY SYSTEMS—HUSBAND/WIFE

These characters are on the phone to each other. Place two chairs back to back on a forty-five degree angle to create the illusion of distance.

Husband: I just checked in.
Wife: How was the flight?
Husband: Bad food. Good movie.
Wife: I miss you.
Husband: I miss you too...
Wife: I feel so alone when you're not here.
Husband: Did you lock the doors and turn on the
    Security system?
Wife: Yep.
Husband: I'll be home tomorrow night.
Wife: I'll be here.

Appendix 3:
Sample Spokesperson Commercials

CHARACTER SPOKES COPY SAMPLES

The first five samples of character spokes copy is the full copy for the commercials that are analyzed and used as examples in Chapter 11.

Day care

Mom: You ask me how I feel about being a working parent? Well, since I've started working, I've had a jumble of feelings--glad, sad, and everything in-between. But now we're doing just fine, thank you. I've got a good job and Kelly's got ChildCare. I wanted the best childcare possible so when I read that ChildCare was offering a free day, I made an appointment for a visit and I liked what I saw. So did Kelly. Do yourself and your child a favor. Call ChildCare and arrange for a free visit. You'll be glad you did.

Beauty soap

Woman: Ever notice how fast things change when they change? Like one day you're your parents' single daughter in Chicago, then all of a sudden you're their unmarried daughter. And you don't even know when it happened. Or all of your life your skin's oily...and then all of a sudden it's dry. And instead of using your boyfriend's green and white soap... you're carrying your own in your purse... 'Course my dry skin's a lot easier to deal with than my oily skin ever was. But then again...what isn't? Growing up does have certain advantages.

Wine

Man: I've spent my entire adult life pretending
     to know something about wine. I don't! Those
     labels are all Greek to me whether they're
     French or Italian. So tonight I stopped
     pretending and started serving what I know
     and what I like. California wine. Pure,
     natural, delicious taste and no fooling.

Highway Safety

Patrolman: A policeman never forgets the first
     highway fatality he sees. Mine was eleven
     years ago. It's something you never forget.
     I had a six-year-old die in my arms. It
     still wakes me up some nights. She'd be
     about seventeen today if her mother had made
     her wear a safety belt. Wearing safety belts
     can save a third of the fifty thousand
     highway fatalities every year. All I know is
     in those eleven years I've never once
     unbuckled a dead man.

Breakfast cereal

Dad: My son's home from college not one day and
     already with the questions. "Since when have
     you been eating Merrios," he asked.
"Since I learned nutrition can be simple," I
     told him.
"Look, you're confused. Everybody's confused. So
     make your life simple," I told him. "Merrios
     is low-sugar, whole-grain oats with all the
     oat bran. Nutrition made simple."
Phi Beta Kappa and he still can learn a thing
     from his old man.

EXTRA CHARACTER SPOKES COPY SAMPLES

Emily (*talking on the phone*):
     I've seen his picture.
     He's Monica's brother.
     I've heard great things.
     And tomorrow is our first date!
     (pause)

I will, it's our first date!
He'll be here at 6.
(pause)
Make it 8? ...why 8?
(pause)
It's dark by 8? So what?
The night will hide my flakes?
I can't have dandruff, I shampoo everyday!!
(pause)
Regular shampoos don't, even if you use 'em everyday???
(pause)
Clean & Shiney??? You use Clean & Shiney?
You don't have dandruff.
Got it!

Ketchup

Mom: What a day! My kid was late for school and ran out of the house before breakfast.
My husband ran for the bus.
I ran to the supermarket. Ran back to let in the plumber...
Ran to the cleaners...All day long I've been running...
...running...
And I said to myself, "I must be crazy. Why am I running?
Why are we all running? Why don't we <u>slow down</u>?"
Look at Slowz Ketchup here.
Slowz never runs.
That's why it tastes so good.
So why don't we all take a tip from this demonstration.
Stop running and slow down...
Like Slowz.

"Mad Willie"

Willie: They call me a psycho. They don't understand. My friends say "Willie, let's go have some fun." I say, "My fun's right here." My car's more than a car. It lets me express who I am...It's my freedom. My girlfriend

Theresa, she said, "Willie, it's me or the car!" Now I got all the time in the world to spend under the hood. I never forgot what my father told me: "Kid--ya want the best outta your car, trust the guys who help you put the best into it."

Glass cleaner

Woman: I have a job now. So my husband said we need some help with the housework. But every time we tried to hire someone, they'd say "I don't do windows." Well, GoodGlass does windows without streaking--and it does appliances, cabinets, countertops.And just look how it cleans chrome. Who says you can't find good help anymore?
GoodGlass. It does windows and a whole lot more.

Luxury car

Accountant: I'm Bob Conroy, president of my own accounting firm.
Two things about accountants I want to cover today.
A--Accountants are not boring
and B--we're pretty sharp when it comes to dollars and cents.
Proof of both--I just bought a Presidential RideMaster. Gorgeous, huh?
With cash rebate and option package bonus it was only eleven and change.
Like I said, we accountants are very smart-- and definitely not boring.

Pain reliever

Cowboy: Cowboyin' ain't nothin' special. Just plain, hot, dusty work. Yeah, that ol' sun can get to beatin' down so hard gives you a headache. Whoo!
You keep some Delamin around if you know what's good for ya.
More medicine, yeah. But no more headache, that's like a cool drink down a dry throat.

Androgynous Spokes Copy Samples

"Don't Worry"

Spokesperson: If you color your hair by the time it grows from here to here, you've colored it 16 times. But don't worry. Just stop coloring your hair and start color-conditioning it. With new Conditioning Creme HairColor...a thick luxurious creme that's saturated with conditioners so your hair actually gets silkier every time you color it...while you color it. Better than Ultress. Better than Preference. Better than Nice'n Easy. The better the condition the better the color. Don't just color your hair. Color condition it with Permanent HairColor. This is big news.

Weight loss

Presenter: Science is always searching for better ways to lose weight. That's why these studies, conducted at clinics like this and published in medical journals, are so important. They prove you can lose more weight with Dexitrol. Doctors compared people on diets alone... to people who dieted and also used Dexitrol. The Dexitrol people lost fifty percent more weight. Fifty percent. Dexitrol helps you eat less and lose more. Diet with Dexitrol and lose more weight.

Flea control

Spokesperson: You won't get rid of fleas in your home... unless you kill them on your pets at the same time. And that's why the makers of Fight Back invented Fight Back Flea Control System. It includes a new pet spray... designed to work together...with a new Fight Back flea fogger. So while the fogger...is killing fleas in your home...the spray is killing them on your pets. The Fight Back Flea Control System kills fleas in your home and on your pets at the same time.

Bowl cleaner

Voice-over: When the makers of Cleanol products set out to create the world's best automatic bowl cleaner...they had to concentrate! That's how Power Bowl was born. Power Bowl is a giant of a bowl cleaner...but it's small! It's concentrated...to last up to 4 months! But the big news is...Power Bowl cleans so thoroughly... leaves the water so clear...you hardly ever have to brush! Get the only automatic bowl cleaner from the makers of Cleanol Products...Power Bowl. Get giant-sized cleaning...from the little yellow box!

Pain reliever

Spokesperson: Here's a quiz you may fail.

Which of these pain relievers can most people take without stomach upset? If you only picked this one, you're wrong! Most people can take Extra-Strength Protectorin or Extra-Strength Tylenol without stomach upset. Which has the strongest dosage you can buy? They both do. Now...which contains the pain reliever doctors recommend most? If you said both... you're wrong...only Extra-Strength Protectorin contains aspirin... the pain reliever doctors recommend most. Which is for you? We think... Extra-Strength Protectorin.

Camera

Spokesperson: Watch me. You are seeing something you've never seen before. The most advanced photographic system in the world at work. It's the new Spectrum. With a brilliantly designed new lens system and the most accurate auto focus of any camera in the world. It gives you pictures so sharp, so life-like they're virtually indistinguishable from compact thirty-five millimeter. So real, in fact, we've shot this entire commercial, one shot at a time, with the Spectrum. We take your pictures seriously.

Makeup

Spokesperson: There's one makeup that is famous for what it won't do. Natural Beauty Oil-Free Makeup. No oil. So it won't shine up. No oil, so it won't clog your pores. No oil. No shine. No problems. It's one makeup that can't feel heavy or greasy...ever! It's oil-free...so it won't clog your pores, and it won't shine up...so you stay beautiful all day long. Natural Beauty Oil-Free Makeup. It's famous for what it won't do.

Medical care

Spokesperson: The Senior HealthCare Plan I'm going to tell you about might seem too good to be true. But it's true all right. It's the HMO Medicare Plan. And our telephone number is right at the bottom of your screen...(you'll probably want to call and ask questions). This is the HMO Headquarters right outside of Pittsburgh. It's here that a Medicare Plan was developed that gives you more benefits than you now get with Medicare and your supplemental insurance combined...but for no more money than you now pay for Medicare alone. It covers unlimited visits to a private doctor in his office. Even for routine checkups. With no deductibles. No cutoffs. And no complicated forms to fill out.

Magazine

Woman: Are you ready to fall in love, again? The current issue of *Femininity* magazine has some surprising answers for you. *Femininity* truly understands what a woman wants to know. This month you'll also find...why some women attract more men, and others don't. Helpful advice for the woman who's suddenly single. What to do if you're having trouble making new friends. And, how to improve your relationship with your mate, especially if it isn't what it used to be.
(voice-over) You'll find it all, only in *Femininity*.

Appendix 4:
Samples of Acting Styles in Commercial Copy

FILM-STYLE COMMERCIALS

Film-Style Character Spokes

This is the story of a tough teacher made teary-eyed by the card her student sends, and thereby illustrates the "emotional power" of the product. The emotional impact of the card upon the character's tough exterior allows us to see the soft and deeply caring interior.

```
Teacher: I used to get her so mad at me in
    class. I thought she was going to spit
    thumbtacks. She was right; I was tough on
    her. I knew what she had in that brain of
    hers. The trick was how to challenge her,
    how to make her... curious.
I just got a card from her. Listen to this:
    "Thanks for seeing someone inside me I
    didn't know was there." Some days it all
    seems worthwhile. (Bell rings) Well, back to
    the pits. I have another kid coming along
    very nicely.
```

Film-Style Slice-of-Life

This spot often deceives my student actors. Even though Claire talks about the product, she never serves it, nor does Leo eat any. There is no demonstration—the soup is a metaphor for Claire's affection for Leo. This is a love story about two shy people who finally connect in this moment, demonstrating the advertiser's attempt to equate feelings—love and caring—with the product.

```
Leo: Oh hi, Claire, how have you been?
Waitress: Fine, Leo, fine... I missed you last
    week...
Leo: Oh yeah, well I've been putting in a little
    overtime.
```

```
Waitress: You know, Leo, sometimes I think you
         work too hard... How about a nice delicious
         bowl of Soup.
Leo: Soup?
Waitress: Sure, it says right here in Reader's
         Digest that soup's one of the most
         nutritious foods you can eat... Why chicken
         noodle soup is just the right thing for a
         big strapping guy like yourself.
Leo: You know something, Claire, we never seem
         to have enough time to talk...
Waitress: I know, Leo, I know.
```

Film-Style MOS

This MOS illustrates how a headache can ruin a great day. It tells us nothing about the product.

You're walking down the street. It's a beautiful day. You feel terrific. You discover you don't feel so terrific. You discover you have a headache. You discover you have a bad headache.

Sitcom-Style Commercials

Sitcom-Style Character Spokes

This story is a classic "before" and "after." The character's story demonstrates the power of the product. It even triumphed over her sister's kids. Even though the character is telling us about a past event, the story is based on facts and a demonstration, rather than an "emotional" experience for the character.

```
Sister: So I'm at my sister's, trying to keep
         her kids from killing each other, right, and
         I get this headache that's killing me. So I
         look in her medicine cabinet and all she has
         is Medivil. Medivil?! But the box says its
         Ibuprofen--that's what's in Motrin and my
         headache said, "Try anything!" Well, that
         Medivil. In no time my headache was gone--
         History! Now my medicine cabinet has
         Medivil, too. For my sister's surprise
         visits--with the kids.
```

Sitcom-Style Slice-of-Life

In the "time passes" segment, where the announcer speaks, the camera shows a demonstration of the hero-product against its competitors. When we come back to our story, the WaterClear dishes are being unloaded from the dishwasher.

Woman #1 is now confident enough about her dishes to have invited Liz "perfect" Roberts for coffee. She felt like a failure, she now feels like a winner.

```
1st Woman: I felt like a complete failure!
2nd Woman: Why? Does she make more money than you?
1st Woman: The first time I see Liz "perfect"
    Roberts in ten years and what happens?
2nd Woman: I don't know. What?
1st Woman: We're about to let our hair down over a
    cup of coffee--I open the dishwasher... to get
    out the espresso cups... and there they are!
2nd Woman: There who is?
1st Woman: Not who--what. Spots. Spots on
    everything. I felt like I was back in the
    college cafeteria!
2nd Woman: That bad? Yuck. Look, maybe she didn't
    notice.
1st Woman: Hah! But never mind her. I noticed!
Announcer: Noticing spots all over your dishes?
    That's when you should try WaterClear. The
    detergent with sheeting action... to get your
    dishes virtually spotless.
1st Woman: WaterClear's fabulous. These dishes have
    success written all over them.
2nd Woman: Right, but will Liz ever see them?
(Doorbell rings.)
1st Woman (gesturing): Uh huh.
Announcer: WaterClear. For virtually spotless dishes.
```

Sitcom-Style MOS
The following demonstration of the terrible taste of soap residue takes you from happy to embarrassed.

You are giving a dinner party for your husband's new boss. You pick up your water glass and take a drink. It tastes terrible. It's soap residue. Your dishwasher soap failed.

"HONEYMOONERS"-STYLE COMMERCIALS

"Honeymooners"-Style Character Spokes
The girl speaking does not represent the product, Cindy does. Therefore, our character is allowed to have dark emotions, to be envious and hate Cindy—but, only if she is a funny character like Lucille Ball. We are allowed to laugh at her!

```
Friend: Don't you hate those annoying friends who
    always know about hot new trends before you do?
```

Like my girlfriend Cindy. Tall, blonde, capped
    teeth. Perfect. She came up to me yesterday.
I was on my tenth diet soda that morning and
    Cindy hands me this new drink called Free.
"What is it?" I politely inquire.
"Where have you been!" she shouts. "It's Free
    and it's absolutely faaaaabulous."
"Light on calories for our tiny waists," she
    says all smug and unnaturally thin. So, as
    soon as she breezed out of the room, I snuck
    a little sip.
Surprise, surprise.
It tasted wonderful, and I hated Cindy more than
    ever.

"Honeymooners"-Style Slice-of-Life

Again, this couple is not the couple that uses the product. They are the
snooping neighbors with binoculars. They are meant to be comedic stereotypes. We should laugh at the husband and wife.

Wife: George! Guess what they have now!
Husband: Stop snooping.
Wife: Some new kitchen bag. With a drawstring!
    It closes with just one pull!
Husband: No kitchen bag has a drawstring!
Wife: New Clinch Sacks do.
Husband: Clinch Sacks?
Wife: And look, George! Clinch Sacks make closing
    and carrying trash bags a cinch, too.
Husband: Oh, you mean because they have this
    drawstring built right in?
Wife: That's right.
Husband: Gimme those glasses.
Announcer: New Clinch Sack Trash and Tall kitchen
    bags. Just one pull makes it a cinch.
Wife: Show-offs.

"Honeymooners"-Style MOS (An Express Mail Service)

The obvious display of disinterest in the needs of their customers by these
characters will be contrasted against the hero-service. These workers are definitely chosen to give broad comedic interpretations of lazy dumbbells.

The dispatch room of the client's competitor. Workers slowly load packages on
an even slower conveyer belt. The workers all look bored and a little dumb.

Appendix 5:
Sample Commercial Storyboard

If you're fortunate, you'll have a chance to read the storyboards for a commercial before you audition for a role in that commercial. Here is the Steve and Barbara slice-of-life scene in storyboard form.

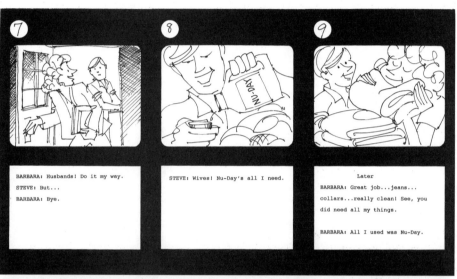

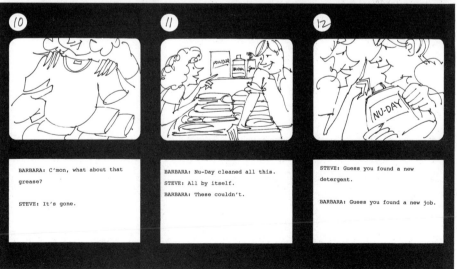

Appendix 6:
SAG Advice Regarding Agents

Screen Actors Guild provides its members with the following business warnings and tips.

1. Make sure your agent is franchised with SAG before signing an agency contract or accepting verbal representation.

2. Agent's clients lists are available to SAG members for inspection at the SAG's Agency Department.

3. All changes in your SAG agency listing must be made in writing—we cannot accept them by phone. Always include your Social Security number.

4. "Verbal" contracts (where there is no written agency contract in existence, or while new contracts are being prepared) can be filed with SAG by the performer sending SAG a written letter stating that they are represented by XYZ Talent agent for XYZ field of representation; or by the Talent Agent using the Client Confirmation Form. This information will remain in SAG's computer system until we are advised, in writing, to remove and/or change such information.

5. Improper behavior by an agent should be reported to SAG immediately. These matters are handled confidentially. Your name is never used without your consent.

6. SAG does not have jurisdiction over print work and/or modeling.

7. With respect to all moneys for TV and Theatrical compensation, the agent has three (3) business days from the time the agency receives the money; and with respect to moneys received as compensation for television commercials, five (5) business days from the time the agent receives the money from the employer. Concerning payments received from an employer drawn on a financial institution located in a state other than the state in which the agent's office is located, the time for the agent to pay over to the actor is seven (7) calendar days.

8. Make sure that you are using the SAG form contract when signing with an agency, and never sign contracts that contain blank spaces or are missing information.

9. SAG does not regulate Personal Managers.

QUESTIONS AND ANSWERS ABOUT THE BUSINESS

SAG distributes the following information, which they get from the Los Angeles Office of the Consumer Protection Division of the Federal Trade Commission.

QUESTION: What is the difference between a legitimate talent agency and one whose purpose is to separate you from your money?

ANSWER: The legitimate talent agency does not charge a fee payable in advance for registering you, for resumes, for public relations services, for screen tests, for photographs, for acting lessons, or for many other services used to separate you from your money. If you are signed as a client by a legitimate talent agency, you will pay such agency nothing until you work and then 10 percent of your earnings as a performer—but nothing in advance. Legitimate talent agencies normally do not advertise for clients in newspaper classified columns nor do they solicit through the mail.

QUESTION: Are legitimate talent agencies licensed by the State of California?

ANSWER: Yes. Such talent agencies are licensed by the State as Talent Agents and most established agencies in the motion picture and television film field are also franchised by the Screen Actors Guild. You should be extremely careful of any talent agency not licensed by the State.

QUESTION: What about personal managers and business managers?

ANSWER: There are well established firms in the business of personal management and business management but such firms in the main handle established artists and they do not advertise for newcomers, nor promise employment.

QUESTION: What about photographers?

ANSWER: If a purported talent agent seeks to send you to a particular photographer for pictures, what should you do? Hold your wallet tight and run for the nearest exit. Chances are he's phony and he makes his money by splitting the photographer's fee. If you need photographs, choose your own photographer. Better still, try another agent. But don't pay anything in advance.

Further Reading

The following is a selected list of acting texts, with publication information and comments. All the acting books I have mentioned are included here, as well as some others which actors would do well to know about.

Acting for the Camera, Tony Barr (HarperCollins, 1986).
A professional guide to an in-depth understanding of the camera and movie-scene playing.

Acting in Film, Michael Caine (Applause Theatre Books, 1990).
An entertaining and surprisingly astute look into film acting and the actor. Practical, enlightening, and right on the money.

Acting in Television Commercials for Fun and Profit, Squire Fridell (Harmony Books, 1980).
An excellent "how-to" survey book for the beginner.

Audition, Michael Shurtleff (Bantam Books, 1978).
This should be read once a year by every actor; still the definitive text.

A Challenge for the Actor, Uta Hagen (Macmillan, 1991).
Step-by-step exercises and techniques to be used in the presentation of a role.

Fearless Presenting, Eric Maisel, Ph.D. (Back Stage Books, 1997).
A self-help workbook for anyone who needs strategies for mastering performance anxiety, or "stage fright."

Improvisation for the Theatre: A Handbook of Teaching and Directing Techniques, Viola Spolin (Northwestern University Press, 1983).
The book is rich, specific, useful, and fun. Excellent for teachers.

Respect for Acting, Uta Hagen with Haskel Frankel (Macmillan, 1973).
A fine book filled with descriptions of sense memory and emotional memory exercises, concentrating on the physical details of characterization.

Sanford Meisner on Acting, Sanford Meisner and Dennis Longwell (Random House, 1987).
Though deceptive in its simplicity, this book is thorough in its focus on finding the actor within you through your concentration on your partner.

The Technique of Acting, Stella Adler (Bantam Books, 1988).
A straightforward, step-by-step, concise, practical, and comprehensive acting technique, with a deep understanding of human behavior. Surprisingly insightful.

Glossary

The following words are a few of the more important terms you may run into when you begin working in commercials.

Back light: used without front lighting, back lights create a silhouette. Used with key lights (front lighting), the back lights help to alleviate shadows.

Blending: a description of a speech technique in which the actor blends the individual words of a thought group together.

Button: the gesture and/or line that ends a scene or monologue.

Callback: the second audition, and any further auditions, for a job in commercials, theater, or film.

Close-up: a film shot in which only the head and shoulders of the actor appear.

Cold reading: an audition with written dialogue where the actors are given little or no time to prepare.

Copy: the script for a commercial.

Copywriter: the writer hired by the client or the advertising agency to create the script for the commercial.

Cutaway: a film editing term which means the film cuts from one scene and connects to another piece of film from another scene.

Fade out (in, up, or down): a film editing term that describes how we move from one shot to another. A fade is a slow change of light level up or down which is the same as in and out.

Fill light: lights focused to fill in the areas on the set not lit by the key light.

Frame: the border of the television monitor. It surrounds the picture.

Go-see: a modeling term for going and seeing photographers who are choosing models.

Hero-product: the client's product, the star of the shoot.

Key light: the main source of light on a set or person.

Mark: the mark on the studio floor that indicates where the actor should stand; usually indicated by colored tape.

Monitor: the television set that is attached to the camera and shows what is being shot *as* it is being shot.

MOS: a commercial shot without recording sound.

On-camera: acting done in front of a camera for future replay on film or tape.

Out-takes: scenes or segments of film that are cut from the final editing of a filmed project.

Pick-up: a film shot of the same scene using a different camera angle than the long shot.

Plosives: the plosive consonant sounds B, P, D, T, G, K. They are made by stopping the breath with the lips, the tip of the tongue, or the back of the tongue, stopping the breath and then exploding it.

Post-production: all the work done on a commercial after it is shot—the editing, musical scoring, and duplicating, for example.

PSAs: Public Service Announcements. Commercials produced to raise awareness of public issues such as drug abuse or literacy.

Residuals: payments made to actors for client's right to re-use commercials.

SAG: Screen Actors Guild. The union of film actors organized under the AFL-CIO in 1933. Its jurisdictions are feature films, most commercials, many industrials, and prime time programs.

Scoring: A term for marking copy. It organizes thoughts and reminds the reader of inflections.

Sitcom: abbreviation for situation comedy; a television entertainment genre.

Slate: a spoken introduction that identifies the performer at the beginning of each take; you may be asked to slate your agent's name as well as your own.

Slice-of-life: advertising jargon for a scene.

Spit-bucket: a bucket that is provided on the set for actors to spit unswallowed food into.

Spokesperson: the actor or announcer who speaks for the product.

Spot: another word for commercial.

Stereotype: a person, group, or event considered to typify an unwavering pattern or manner.

Take: a performance captured on film.

TVQ: a rating system of performers' recognizability and likability.

Voice-over: the voice of the actor that is heard over the picture. The actor is not seen.

Index

Monologue format. *See* Spokesperson

MOS (minus optical strip), 62–63, 64, 76–87, 166–167
  film-style, 87, 179
  "Honeymooners"-style, 181
  sitcom-style, 87, 180
MOS response, 85–86
Movement, at MOS audition, 82–83
Multiple camera technique, 47–48
Music video form, 63

Naturalistic acting, 69
Nonlinear process, in filming, 47
Nonverbal communication, 28–30
Nursery rhymes, story through, 30–32

Objectives, 97–98
Obstacles, 112
On-camera acting, 16
One-line commercials, 88–94
Opening beat, 98–99, 101–102, 116–117
Outward communication, 86

Pace, 132–133
Packard, Vance, 22
Performance anxiety, 154
Physicalization, 43–44
Physical "landmines," 138–140
Plosive consonants, 126
Plot, 80
Posture, 122, 123
Precis, 130
Preconceptions, 15
Presentation, 144–146
Presentational speech, 122, 123–124
Product(s)
  feelings about, 133–134
  as part of story, 102
Product trap, 106–107
Projection, sizing needs for, 49, 51
Props, at MOS audition, 83
Psychological "landmines," 141–142
Punctuation, 128–129

Readiness, 143–150
Reading people, 32–33
Real character spokesperson, 95–96
Real people interviews, 63
Real space, 48–51
Relationship, of characters, 112–113
Relaxation, 41–42
Residuals, 21
Response
  acting, 42–43, 90
  of consumers, 23

MOS, 85–86
Résumés, 148
Retelling script, 104–105
Rewards, 16–19
Richardson, Jack, 29
Rolston, Matthew, 159
Ross Reports, 150
Roy, Rene, 21

Scene format. *See* Slice-of-life
Schein, Gideon Y., 143
Schramm, David, 36
Scoring, 127–129
Screen Actors Guild (SAG), 9, 17–18, 21–22, 149
  advice of, regarding agents, 184–185
Scripts, 24, 57–58. *See also* Copy
  analysis of, 25, 63–64
  retelling, 104–105
  without dialogue, 62–63, 76–87
Sellers, 70–71, 72, 118
Selling, acting versus, 15–16, 23–25
Set, working on, 93–94
Set-up, 46
Sex appeal, 20–21
Shurtleff, Michael, 20, 25, 28, 100, 112, 150
Silent dialogue, 37–38
"Silly Goosedom" device, 105
Single camera technique, 46–47
Single shot, 50
Sitcom-style commercials, 69–73, 75, 116–118, 179–180
Sizing, of projection needs, 49, 51
Skills, acting, 146
  four basic, 41–44
Slice-of-life, 60, 63, 64, 109–119, 168–170
  film-style, 178–179
  "Honeymooners"-style, 181
  sitcom-style, 116–118, 179–180
Sound, of feeling, 92
Space
  audition, 53–56
  real, communication over, 48–51
Speech
  conversational, 120–123
  presentational, 122, 123–124
  voice and, 124–127
Speed, of audition, 24–25
Spokes-model, 20–21
Spokesperson, 60–62, 63
  androgynous, 61, 120–135, 175–177
  character. *See* Character spokesperson
Spolin, Viola, 43
Spontaneity, 89

JOAN SEE began acting in commercials thirty years ago and continues auditioning and acting in them today. She has appeared on-camera in hundreds of commercials, including the debut spots for Final Net, Lanacaine, Tegrin, and Pepcid AC. She was also the off-camera voice of Stouffer's frozen foods, Total cereal, and Avon. A graduate of Hofstra University with degrees in English, Speech, and Theater, Ms. See received her professional training from Sanford Meisner and Wynn Handman. She has performed in live television, in soap opera, and on the stage.

In the early 1980s, when she took up teaching, Ms. See founded Actors in Advertising and Three of Us Studios. Actors in Advertising became the School for Film and Television, which specializes in training actors for performance in those media and now offers a two-year film-acting conservatory program accredited by the National Association of Schools of Theater. This program and the School's summer acting intensives for high school students attract young actors from all over the country.

Joan See has also served her profession as a board member and first vice president of the New York branch of the Screen Actors Guild.